P9-AQC-361

ROYAL COMMISSIONS OF INQUIRY

ROYAL COMMISSIONS OF INQUIRY

The Significance of Investigations in British Politics

By

HUGH McDOWALL CLOKIE

and

J. WILLIAM ROBINSON

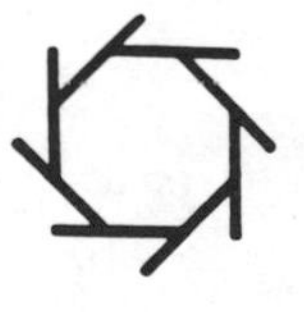

1969

OCTAGON BOOKS

New York

Reprinted 1969
by special arrangement with Stanford University Press

OCTAGON BOOKS
A DIVISION OF FARRAR, STRAUS & GIROUX, INC.
19 Union Square West
New York, N. Y. 10003

LIBRARY OF CONGRESS CATALOG CARD NUMBER: 70-86274

Printed in U.S.A. by
TAYLOR PUBLISHING COMPANY
DALLAS, TEXAS

PREFACE

This monograph concerns the significance and present status of Royal Commissions of Inquiry in relation to British politics. The study was undertaken because of the recurring interest in Royal Commissions. The scanty literature on the subject displays vagueness and uncertainty, as well as definite error and contradiction, not only as to the origins of these bodies, but also in regard to their institutional significance. With the exception of two essays in professional journals (W. H. Moore, "Executive Commissions of Inquiry," in *Columbia Law Review,* Vol. XIII [1913]; and H. F. Gosnell, "British Royal Commissions of Inquiry," in *Political Science Quarterly,* XLIX [1934]) and occasional paragraphs in the standard works of reference, no special attention has hitherto been directed to the Royal Commission as a notable example of the wise combination of fact-finding and policy-forming in the modern state. The only book devoted to the subject is that of an embittered opponent of the nineteenth-century Whig Reformers (J. Toulmin Smith, *Government by Commissions Illegal and Pernicious* . . . . [1849]). The attention paid to this author may seem out of proportion to his merit; but it is justified by the lack of other works and by the fact that he systematizes much of the criticism which has been bestowed on Royal Commissions of Inquiry.

The roots of Commission procedure extend far back into Norman times; and in the evolution of this method of inquiry the innumerable Commissions have been successively the instrument of King, Parliament, and Cabinet. The present volume is not intended as a complete handbook to all these inquiries past and present. Specific Commissions have been dealt with only in so far as they possess particular significance for the development of this type of investigation.

Despite contemporary opinion to the contrary, it is our conclusion that the Golden Age of Royal Commissions is past and that newer devices and processes are rapidly superseding this venerable agency.

Acknowledgment is made to Doubleday, Doran and Company, Inc., for permission to reprint the selection from Mr. A. P. Herbert's *Mild and Bitter,* which first appeared in *Punch.* And it is with great pleasure that we acknowledge the receipt of helpful advice and criticism from Professor E. M. Sait with respect to an early draft of the first part of this work.

H. McD. C.
J. W. R.

STANFORD UNIVERSITY, CALIFORNIA
June 30, 1937

TABLE OF CONTENTS

LIST OF TABLES

CHART

ROYAL COMMISSIONS OF INQUIRY

CHAPTER I

PLACE OF ROYAL COMMISSIONS OF INQUIRY IN BRITISH GOVERNMENT

The question is to discover not what governments prescribe, but what they ought to prescribe.—LORD ACTON

The clearest and most direct way to minimise conflict is to organise better information upon which to base decisions.—H. J. LASKI

FUNCTION IN PREPARATION FOR LEGISLATION

The use of Royal Commissions of Inquiry in England is consecrated by antiquity and in modern times is dictated by necessity. In the nineteenth century—which was the heyday of the Royal Commission—these agencies were the chief instruments of governmental investigation and preparation for the numerous innovations in social and industrial policy. Today the supremacy of Royal Commissions as a method of inquiry has been challenged by the creation of several other organs of investigation, but they are still utilized at the rate of two or three a year for the ascertainment of facts on important topics, for the airing of certain types of grievances, and for the consideration of possible policies on outstanding political and social questions of the day.

As a phase, and a very important phase of governmental investigations, Royal Commissions can, of course, be coextensive with the entire sphere of state action both in the government's internal organization and in its relation to the citizen. There is thus an infinite possibility of the uses to which the investigative function may be put. Generally speaking, however, investigations have had three major purposes: (1) the consideration of legislative policy; (2) inquiry into the activities of the administrative departments; and (3) inquiry into social conditions. It is in the first of these three—as an agency of legislative preparation—that the British Royal Commission has attained its greatest scope and reputation.

No special philosophy of the nature of law or of the purpose of legislation is requisite for an appreciation of the part played by Royal Commissions in the preparation of legislation. Whether the state should serve chiefly as a policing agency, as an arbitrator between disputants, as an organ for harmonizing conflicting interests, or as the supervisor of "social engineering" makes no difference to the usefulness of this method of social inquisition. The utility of the Commission procedure is in no way connected with theories and doctrines; Royal Commissions have never been offered as a political panacea, as have many other political devices. But Commissions have, on the contrary, been adopted as a practical mechanism for certain fairly definite reasons in each case of their use. So long as these reasons continue to prevail, this instrumentality for gaining special knowledge and consideration of governmental policies seems likely to continue.

Nevertheless, the following considerations may be offered as of importance in the discussion of the place of Royal Commissions in the legislative process. In the first place, Parliament (to say nothing of other legislative assemblies) suffers from serious defects and deficiencies. As a body representative of the nation for which it is to make new and revise old laws, Parliament, at its best, is both too inexpert and too preoccupied with transient political considerations to undertake the serious and lengthy analysis of many problems the wise solution of which demands trained minds, impartial judgment, and disinterested study. Neither Upper nor Lower Chamber can by any stretch of the imagination be regarded as composed of the quintessence of national wisdom. Each House possesses its own peculiarities; but, as is natural in modern political assemblies, membership is rarely more than a test of expertness in electoral procedure. Whatever social sagacity may be found in legislatures is largely incidental and adjunctive; it is certainly not an inherent appurtenance thereof.

A second defect of the composition of Parliament lies in the nature of its selection. Representation in the House of Commons is based upon a geographic foundation of territorial constituencies, and since local residence of members is neither insisted on nor practiced to any considerable degree, there is no assurance that the national distribution of membership will be representative of the special structure of the political communities which constitute the nation. It is not contended that the House of Commons (or Parliament) must be an accurate cross section of the people in order to be truly representative. The point is that in the haphazard system of securing representation the type and experience of prospective legislators exercises an inconsiderable influence upon the process of their selection.

In the third place, the two Houses of Parliament

as political bodies are dominated by partisan considerations. It is not merely that the membership is in its basic sentiments more partisan than the rest of the nation—and the more influential the members the more imbued with partisanship they must be—but that in addition the conditions of English politics restrict to a marked degree the less violent, the better-informed, and the more thoughtful members. The whole process of parliamentary procedure—and in particular its operation—restricts and restrains the inquisitive and inquiring members and enforces a conformity of conduct which is totally destructive of constructive individual thought. Not only do parliamentary discussions assume the form of set debates, the result of which is most frequently predetermined by the party complexion of the chambers, but these very debates are an organized sham-battle between rival teams of debaters, each of which is under a fairly rigid discipline and conducts its argument and proceedings within the limits prescribed by the determination of the party leaders or of the party program. For, as the party conflict progresses, it soon appears that the regimented members of Parliament are by practical necessity under tight bonds of allegiance to the elected leader and to the previously declared party platform. And, needless to say, the party policies, having been adopted for electoral purposes at an earlier date, will have prejudged the most important political issues.

Lastly, among the factors undermining the parliamentary function as the "Grand Inquest of the Nation" is the question of time. On the one hand is the frequent criticism that the members of the House of Commons are too greatly burdened with their private and public affairs to be able to devote the needed arduous and impersonal consideration to organized policy-making; and on the other hand is the fact that pressure of business results in the time of the House being taken up in increasing degree by the Government for its necessary current financial and legislative business. The consequence has been the establishment of a rigid "time-table," the close adherence to which has hindered the participation of private members in both legislation and debate despite the introduction of such devices as the "kangaroo" and "closure by compartments." Legislation has thus become little more than a semblance, perhaps indeed only a parody, of legislative discussion.

The realization of these defects in the parliamentary machine has led to the proposal of numerous remedies, each of which has at one time or other engaged the support of prominent statesmen and publicists. Thus we have had "standing committees" on the American or French order, proposed by the Rt. Hon. Mr. J. R. MacDonald,[1] by Professor H. J. Laski,[2] and by Mr. Ramsay Muir;[3] an economic chamber, endorsed by the Guild Socialists[4] and more recently by the Rt. Hon. Mr. Winston Spencer Churchill;[5] proportional representation, advocated by the

[1] *Parliament and Revolution* (1919), Appendix.

[2] *A Grammar of Politics* (1925), pp. 349, 370, 377 ff.

[3] *How Britain Is Governed* (1930), pp. 229–35. For other suggestions, cf. *Special Report from the Select Committee on Procedure on Public Business* (House of Commons Paper No. 129, 1931); this committee finally reported against them: *Report from the Select Committees on Procedure* (*ibid*, 1932), p. xi.

[4] E.g., G. D. H. Cole, *Self-government in Industry* (1919).

[5] *Parliamentary Government and Economic Problem* (Romanes Lecture, 1930).

Liberal party;[6] and devolution, urged by numerous groups in the past twenty years.[7]

As previously stated, Royal Commissions have been a practical device, not a panacea, and have been employed because they have been found effective methods of tapping new sources of information, of gaining access to political opinion of a nonpartisan origin, and of imparting an expert quality to the amateurish game of government. The efficiency of Royal Commissions in these aspects, coupled with the opportunity they provide for careful weighing of all sides of a problem over a period of months or even of years, has occasionally enabled them to embody the merits attributed to the Ideal Senate: a model representative character, learned and inquiring impartiality, and a practical combination of the search for justice and the steps by which it is to be attained.

FUNCTION IN INVESTIGATION OF THE EXECUTIVE

The second purpose for which governmental investigations are used—namely, inquiry into the conduct of the executive departments and into the incidence of administrative regulations upon the individual—does not afford to Royal Commissions the wide scope and publicized opportunity for broad policy discussion that the legislative use allows. This does not necessarily mean that the existing institutions and procedures are of so complete and adequate

[6] *The Liberal Way* (1934), Pt. iii.

[7] A resolution was carried in the House of Commons in 1919 approving the creation of subordinate legislatures in the United Kingdom. It was followed by a conference, presided over by the Speaker, which offered suggestions which have never been carried out except in the case of Ireland. *Conference on Devolution* (Cmd. 692, 1920). Cf. W. H. Chiao, *Devolution in Great Britain* (1926).

a type as to protect the subject from all forms of maladministration and executive injustice. Rather it implies that such other machinery as does exist has to a large degree prevented the insistent demand for the utilization of the Royal Commission process. Examples of these other forms of interrogating the executive are to be found in parliamentary procedure (such as in the "question hour"), in executive practice (as is seen in the deputations which wait upon the ministerial heads), and in the usual judicial arrangements for the determination of private rights. Nevertheless, it is commonly thought that the protection and safeguarding of the rights of the subject has not kept pace with the extension of governmental interference in the everyday affairs of social and industrial life.

In general, of course, the operation of Cabinet government has been regarded as sufficiently checking the ministers and the administrative departments in the conduct of their duties. Votes of censure, debates upon the estimates for the various services, and the other parliamentary procedures for the public consideration of the conduct of the Government are the regular and constant assertions of the right of the members of Parliament to investigate the course of action in the several governmental agencies. Yet the factors which were enumerated in the preceding pages are influential here also. The very facts of party discipline and of the partisan nature of most parliamentary proceedings tend to discount the serious and sober inquiry into the working of the governmental agencies. The multiplicity of subjects which must be dealt with, the rigorous control which the

Government exercises over the "time-table," and the selective nature of the debates of the estimates[8] do in fact prevent adequate discussion of the problems which a number of people regard as worthy of consideration. The need for adequate discussion has become especially pressing in view of the practice of making legislative enactments in the broadest terms and leaving the details to be filled in by means of departmental regulations which are merely laid upon the table of the House and if unchallenged, as is usually the case, become officially operative.

Royal Commissions have continually been appointed for the purpose of making investigations into the administration of the law. The Royal Commission procedure is so flexible and convenient that occasionally, in the face of insistent demand, the Government finds itself forced to provide, in addition to the usual parliamentary controls, a further method of inquiry into its own conduct or into that of its subordinate officials. It may be admitted that this use of Royal Commission procedure is less regularly resorted to than formerly for the purpose of checking the misconduct of officialdom. There have been cases—and there will probably be similar ones in the future—where the Prime Minister or the Cabinet finds that the best protection against scandal will be the wise display of impartiality shown by the creation of a Commission of Inquiry.[9] But at the

[8] Since it is impossible to discuss each branch of every department, it is customary when the appropriations for a department are being debated for the Opposition to be given the choice of subjects to be dealt with in the limits of the particular "vote."

[9] During the World War the British Government was singularly free from the type of inquisition which continually threatened both the French and the American military administrations. The only inquiry

present time such investigations are not as prominent as in the past. It is not now so frequently within the scope of Commissions to inquire into the existing law and circumstances and to recommend large changes of a legislative nature or perhaps the alteration of administrative regulations.

That Royal Commissions have not shown the same noteworthy and luxuriant growth in the investigation of executive conduct must be held to indicate a serious deficiency in English political institutions. It will be evident of course that Commissions are in their very nature quite transient establishments. They are created *ad hoc* to meet occasional emergencies; and when its immediate task is accomplished a Commission, with its members and their accumulated knowledge (except as published), disintegrates and scatters to the four winds. It is only rarely—and usually in nonadministrative fields — that a Royal Commission may continue indefinitely to perform a task of lasting magnitude, as with the Royal Historical Manuscripts Commission. But for the great majority of investigative commissions their function terminates when their immediate task is performed and their final report presented.

There is a third purpose which is served by the Royal Commission procedure, namely, research into

into the conduct of the war was established by statute to investigate the operations in the Dardanelles and Mesopotamia, and to ascertain "the responsibility of those departments of Government whose duty it has been to minister to the wants of the Forces in those theatres of war." 6 & 7 Geo. V. c. 34, 1916.

More recently investigations of allegations of a "third degree" procedure in police questioning in the Savidge case were undertaken by a Select Committee of the House of Commons, and the comment which this report aroused resulted in the appointment of a Royal Commission on Police Powers and Procedure (*Report,* Cmd. 3297, 1929).

social conditions. The compilation of accurate information by means of the careful sifting of verifiable facts and by the patient ascertainment of the details of various aspects of social problems is undoubtedly a most important antecedent of sound state action upon any current question. Effective public policy can be determined upon only after the facts and circumstances relating to society and to law administration are investigated. Indeed it is evident that every Royal Commission, whether engaged in research for legislative purposes or inquiry into administrative misconduct, must engage in this function of research in order to accomplish its investigative purpose. Yet though the search for pertinent knowledge is common to all the inquiries previously mentioned, there are a large number of investigations which fall outside these two categories and which are by their very nature, scope, and duration particularly noteworthy as examples of this research function apart from their legislative or administrative purposes.

The research, statistical, and informing function of the state has received increasing recognition in recent years. Not only are the annual reports of the departments concerned with trade, industry, education, crime, labor, etc., valuable sources of socio-economic information, but the numerous supervisory and inspectional services of a social and technical nature are regularly publishing the results of special inquiries which departmental experts conduct into various phases of business, industrial, and sociological conditions. Recognition of the importance of this modern function led the Haldane Committee on the Machinery of Government to propose in 1918 the establishment of a special department with a ministerial head to co-ordinate these research activities.[10]

This feature of modern government was almost unknown to the permanent departments of a hundred years ago. Before the establishment of a competent and skilled administrative service and before the Government departments were equipped with the trained and expert personnel which could undertake this investigative function, Royal Commissions of Inquiry were a most useful and an almost necessary device for procuring the statistical and descriptive knowledge required for the legislative changes of the period. Today, however, when the efficiency of the civil services has advanced to a high standard, this need for a special research procedure is less urgent. Yet despite the impressive products of the research facilities of the Government departments and their experts, there still frequently arise occasions on which an additional method of inquiry is advisable. New problems are continually coming to the fore as having been overlooked by the established administrators; new attitudes have to be brought to these investigations; and the collaboration of layman with expert or of politician with administrator has to be effected. In the past, the most satisfactory method of breaking through official self-complacency and of providing inquiries into novel or neglected problems has been the Royal Commission.

LACK OF MACHINERY FOR EXECUTIVE SUPERVISION

On the side, then, of administrative or executive supervision, Great Britain lacks adequate machinery

[10] *Report,* Cd. 9230, 1918, pp. 6, 7, 35. No action followed this recommendation.

for continuous and consistent inspection and investigation. The need for such activity exists in three major fields. There is, first, a decided lack of parliamentary supervision of the departmental organization. With the exception of the political controls which the House of Commons exercises over the Cabinet (and which are exercised in a diminishing degree as time goes on), the legislative supervision over the administration of the policies for which laws have been made and money voted is quite defective. Putting aside the audit by a special committee, which covers only one or two departments each year,[11] the members of the Houses of Parliament have to rest content with the annual exposition of departmental policy offered by the minister concerned and with the undebatable replies given in the "question hour." Moreover, of course, the administration is entirely free from all but journalistic interrogation during the months of each year in which Parliament is not sitting.

The closest control over the administrative function is maintained by the Treasury. Not only does this department, as the watchdog of finance, maintain a close scrutiny of expenditures and receipts, of actual expenses and desired extensions, but also by committee and interdepartmental committees it seeks to maintain that external supervision which is essential for the efficiency and the legitimate conduct of any permanent agency of the state. But even this check has the cardinal defect of being imposed by a professional or administrative organ.

[11] *Special Report from Select Committee in Procedure on Public Business* (H.C. 161, 1931), pp. 377–78, question 3777, etc.

This brings us to the second serious gap in English institutions. It is most important for the well-being of the modern community that the public or its representatives—and by this one means the public which is not organized on a political basis — should be brought into an official and ordered relationship with the administrative bodies of the executive. For, as has often been pointed out, the experience of the civil servant and administrator is at best a secondhand experience. While the state is not directly concerned in the management of public industries but chiefly in the regulation and inspection of industrial life, it is essential that the officials of the state should be constantly informed of the nature and social consequences of the rules which they are applying. The only way that this special social experience of the community can be brought authoritatively and concretely to their attention is by the existence of organs on which the various interests concerned are represented as at least equals of the officials. In the determination of the extent of state intervention in the modern industrial system, there is, as Professor Laski has said, a great need for the organization of additional "institutions of consultation," for "no government can have contact with bodies of men entitled to speak with authority and remain uninfluenced by their views."[12]

The acknowledged success of many of the most important Royal Commissions has been due to the fact that they have provided such an avenue of communication between those officials who attempt to hold themselves quite aloof from the practical con-

[12] H. J. Laski, *Grammar of Politics* (1925), pp. 80, 81.

sequences of state regulation. But, as already remarked, a Royal Commission is a transient body, directing itself usually to the consideration of a single isolated problem and possessing no consciousness of continuity or of obligation to later and wider implications.

Lastly, there must be considered the general legal aspects of the existing rules of common law which have militated against the creation of a state responsibility for injustices arising in the dealings between the government and the individual. Admirable as may be the ancient doctrine that "the King can do no wrong," it is clearly an unwarranted assumption that the rule should be preserved in order to protect the state as well as the servants of the Crown from the just consequences of infringements of the rights of individuals. Although statutory alteration of the law respecting suits against the Crown has been recommended,[13] no action has been taken; and though the more recent investigation of the general question of ministerial powers resulted in the endorsement of the older legal dogmas,[14] the fact remains that the enlargement of state functions shows no signs of abatement, but rather the contrary. Unless provision is made for the establishment of some form of administrative courts, there must be arrangement for a certain measure of civilian participation in the direction and administration of the multitudinous activities of the state.[15]

[13] *Report of Crown Proceedings Committee* (Cmd. 2842, 1927).

[14] *Report of the Committee on Ministers' Powers* (Cmd. 4060, 1932), especially pp. 8, 9, 71–73.

[15] On the place of the expert in government, after declaring that the "expert ought always to provide the materials for a finding, but never

COMMITTEES IN FRANCE AND AMERICA

The use of committees and investigative agencies in other countries has assumed a line of development very different from that of the English commissions. Committees of the Houses of Parliament (except those for private and local bills) occupy quite a secondary place in English parliamentary procedure. It is true that there are in the House of Commons five standing committees; but with the exception of the "Scottish Committee" these committees (the other four designated simply A, B, C, and D) have no specialization of function or of membership, though additional members especially qualified may be added for a particular bill. Each committee takes for discussion and elaboration the bills which are sent to it by the Speaker regardless of subject matter. These bills are nearly always noncontroversial projects (of a nonpolitical nature) which have been accepted in principle by the House at the second reading. The procedure of the House as a Committee of the Whole for the major Government bills of controversial nature has no connection in fact with committee work. It is merely a historic device to simplify discussion and to proceed without the presence of the Speaker.

In France, on the other hand, a most elaborate and rigid system of grand commissions (twenty in number) is established in the Chamber of Deputies.[16]

the finding itself," Laski quotes Sir William Harcourt: "The value of political heads of departments is to tell the officials what the public will not stand." A. G. Gardiner, *Sir William Harcourt,* II, 587, quoted in *Grammar of Politics,* p. 245.

[16] A. J. L. Breton, *Les Commissions et la Réforme de la Procédure Parlementaire* (1922); J. Barthélémy, *Essai sur le Travail Parlementaire et le Système des Commissions* (1934); R. K. Gooch, *The French Parliamentary Committee System* (1935).

Membership is definitely and recognizedly partisan, depending on the size of the parliamentary groups. The committees are permanent, specialized bodies, paralleling the administrative departments, and possessing each its own room, secretariat, and regular meeting time. They serve as the co-ordinating agencies for the Chamber's control over the ministers and departments. Their control extends not only to the oversight of the Administration but even to the preparation of legislation, which includes acceptance or rejection of the Government's program. While this committee system has been admired for its resultant opportunity for legislative supervision and review of administrative policy and practice in a manner far more effective than the parliamentary discussions can ever be, it has undoubtedly contributed in a very definite way to the instability of ministries and so to a weakening of the sense of Cabinet responsibility for the conduct of the administrative departments. In addition to these usual parliamentary commissions, which exist in both Chambers, the French Parliament has found it necessary to establish special inquiries into the conduct of special departments at certain critical times.[17] These parliamentary "inquests," as they are called, have investigated such important cases of maladministration as the Panama Canal scandal and, more recently, the Stavisky swindle and the Paris riots of 1934. It must be noted that these inquests, though parliamentary bodies, differ from the committees in being special *ad hoc* creations composed of parliamentarians to investigate excep-

[17] R. Arnitz, *Les Enquêtes Parlementaires d'Ordre Politique* (1917); P. Bégouin, *Les Commissions d'Enquête Parlementaire* (1931).

tional cases of administrative failure. Their purpose has accordingly been the careful establishment, often on partisan lines, of responsibility for maladministration in the government departments.

It is in the United States that the use of legislative committees has undergone its greatest development.[18] There are several reasons for this. In the first place, the utility of the various English methods of legislative inquiry which were in use one hundred and fifty years ago was naturally evident to the first members of the new federal government. But in addition to this there are some special American reasons for the existing situation. For one thing, the investigating activities of Congress have arisen in the United States in response to the need for an agency capable of holding the Administration to some sort of accountability. This was one of the first uses of inquiries in America; and it is still by far the most important purpose of investigations there.

It is probable that one may trace this activity directly to the "separation of powers" contemplated by the United States Constitution, a separation which almost immediately precipitated a struggle for supremacy between Congress and the President. Investigations, successive Congresses have discovered, may be employed to supplement the power of the purse, the law-making power, and even the power of impeachment. They have unquestionably proved to be a more effective control than mere resolutions requesting information "if compatible with the pub-

[18] *Vide* M. E. Dimock, *Congressional Investigating Committees* (1929); E. J. Eberling, *Congressional Investigations* (1928); L. G. McConachie, *Congressional Committees* (1898); P. D. Hasbrouck, *Party Government in the House of Representatives* (1927).

lic interest." The significance of this procedure is now gaining increased recognition among American writers. "Congress," one observer has said, "does not seek any day by day articulation of its legislative committees and the administrative departments, as in the case of France, but it does exert some *ex post facto* control through its inquisitions."[19]

Further, there has been the influence of another dominant American principle, that of "checks and balances." In addition to the division of the government into executive and legislative departments (to say nothing of the judiciary), the apparently contradictory expectation that the two great divisions of the government would serve to offset each other has been given constitutional recognition by numerous provisions such as the presidential veto and the executive powers of the Senate. The latter in particular, i.e., the right of the Senate to reject appointments and treaties, has given an extensive and thoroughly utilized opportunity for that chamber to indulge in continual scrutiny and criticism of executive conduct. The legislative investigation, it has been said, "is the American method of achieving ministerial responsibility without reducing power. It is one of the checks in a system of checks and balances."[20] The strange consequence is that, though the House of Representatives might be expected to participate on at least equal terms in this critical function, as is the usual case in parliamentary systems, it does not do so to the fullest

[19] L. Rogers, "Legislative Committees," *Encyclopedia of the Social Sciences*, IV (1931), 43.

[20] G. B. Galloway, "The Investigative Function of Congress," *American Political Science Review*, XXI (1927), 65.

degree. The reasons for this appear to flow from its membership and its procedure. The large size of the House, the rigidity of its rules, and the pettiness of its politics have undeniably limited its effectiveness as a critic. On the other hand, the greater prestige of the Senate, arising from its smaller membership, its continuity, the "filibuster," and its special constitutional attributes, has enabled it to concentrate in its own hands the major task of criticism.[21]

Congress, then, has regularly exercised, by means of special investigating committees, its privilege of inquiring into the conduct and working of the executive departments and their officials; and has, it may be remarked, extended these inquisitional activities into many other fields, including Congressional proceedings. Since the earliest of these legislative investigations in 1792, some 285 such inquiries had been launched by 1926. Only three Congresses have been barren of these inquests, and no Administration has been immune from their inspection and criticism.[22]

The principles of separated powers and of checks and balances not only have given Congress less opportunity to control the executive, but have released it from the pressure of the President and the Cabinet.

[21] On this general subject, *vide* L. Rogers, *The American Senate* (1926).

[22] The record of 37 inquiries which were set on foot during the eight years of President Grant's administration was exceeded under President Wilson, when 51 investigations were made during his last two years. All together the Treasury Department has been involved in 54 inquiries, and the Department of the Interior (with special reference usually to the Indian Bureau and the Pension and Patents Offices) has been investigated 41 times. The War, Navy, and Post Office Departments have been subjected to a similar, though less numerous series of inquiries. Even the presidential office has been called to account on some 25 occasions. Galloway, *op. cit.*, p. 48.

Since the President and his Cabinet officers are not present to explain or defend their policies, the Houses of Congress have had to invent other methods of co-ordinating legislative and executive relations. Partly for this reason, legislative committees have become a regular and institutionalized phase of Congressional procedure. The membership of each House is subdivided into a number of permanent committees for the consideration of legislation upon the classified subjects.[23]

Membership on the committees is quite definitely on a party basis, as it is also in the case of the investigating committees. The majority party of each House has approximately the same proportion of members on each committee that the party has "on the floor" of the House. To these committees all bills—whether of public, private, or local nature, and regardless of whether they originate with members of a House or in reality are proposed by the Administration—are sent for discussion and for drafting before being debated in the House where they were presented. The number of bills thus referred is prodigious; but fortunately only a small proportion sees the light of day after being buried in the files of the committees.[24]

Although no necessity for this appears, bills favorably reported by the committees of one House have not only a better chance of enactment than those pushed through without the approval of the com-

[23] The present number of standing committees is 45 in the House of Representatives (with 2 other select committees), and 33 in the Senate (with 11 other special and select committees). *Congressional Directory*, 75th Cong., 1st. Sess., 1937.

[24] About 8,000 bills are introduced each session. Only about one-seventh are acted on, with some 800 becoming law.

mittees but also a greater chance of passage in the other chamber, in which, despite this preparation, they go through a second committee stage. It must not be forgotten that since the Administration participates only by indirect methods in the work of legislative preparation the presidential veto is still an influential factor in restraining the legislative enthusiasm of Congressmen. In his first term (1933–37) President F. D. Roosevelt vetoed as many as 221 bills presented to him by Congress, a number comparable with that (312 vetoes) which earned Cleveland the title of "the Veto President."

Finally, it should be observed that American committees exhibit a definitely partisan and political bias alike in their membership, their proceedings, and their reports. There is none of the British attempt to secure an impartial investigation into the social or economic circumstances of a legislative or administrative policy. There is no pretense of the committee's being expert or impartial in its pursuit of information. Nor do the political purposes assume such a moderate tone as in the French inquests. Instead, among the most obvious features of an American committee are its blatant publicity and its frequent vulgarity. Investigations are conducted on the plane of propaganda. In many cases the inquiries are completed privately before the public hearings begin; the purpose of the hearing therefore is not to get information but to stir up enough public sentiment to facilitate the passage of legislation that has already been determined upon.[25]

[25] *Vide* P. Mallon, *New York Times Magazine,* December 9, 1934, pp. 6–7.

NEED FOR SUPPLEMENTARY AGENCIES

In conclusion, then, it appears that every democratic parliamentary system finds it necessary to establish some form of supplementary institution to aid in the preparation of legislation, to investigate maladministration on the part of the executive, and to protect the citizens at large from unintentional invasion by governmental agencies. In England, owing to the Cabinet system and to the absence of legislative committees, the chief type of investigation for the past hundred years has been the Royal Commission, a mixed organ of experts and laymen. In France, the legislature has usually provided both legislative consultation and occasional inquests into the executive. In America, handicapped in the control of the executive by the absence of a parliamentary Cabinet system, Congressional committees have found a wide extension of functions both in considering legislative bills and in investigating administrative departments.

Bodies comparable to the Royal Commissions have rarely, if ever, been used in France; and only in recent years have they gained any place in America.[26] Royal Commissions are, as a distinguished foreign commentator has declared, "a typically English device for bringing the best brains in the country to

[26] President Hoover seems to have been the first to realize the advisability of executive inquiries. Among the important bodies which he appointed were that on Law Observance and Enforcement, the Advisory Committee on Illiteracy, the Special Commission to Study Conditions in Haiti, the Special Committee for the Study of Education, and the Commission on Conservation and Administration of the Public Domain. These must not be confused with the permanent administrative or regulative commissions which have been utilized to supplement the administrative organization.

bear on great legislative tasks in their very earliest stages; for making self-government effective over topics for which there are as yet no self-governing organs."[27] Imitation, it has been said, is the sincerest form of flattery. The fact that such commissions are not usual in America makes all the more significant the unofficial and private attempts to copy this institution, as seen in the semipublic inquiries into the Steel Strike of 1919 by the Inter-Church World Movement of America, into Social Trends (1933), and into National Policy in International Economic Relations (1934). That these investigations have been undertaken purely for informational or educational purposes without any immediate expectation of legislative consequences is a further tribute to the general method of nonpartisan inquiry of which the Royal Commission is the chief exemplar.

[27] W. Dibelius, *England* (1930), p. 253.

CHAPTER II

EARLY DEVELOPMENT

In societies, as in living bodies, increase of mass is habitually accompanied by increase of structure.—HERBERT SPENCER

RELATION TO THE CROWN

Governmental investigations in England (i.e., those of nonjudicial and nonadministrative character) fall into two major categories: executive and parliamentary. The executive investigations are conducted either by Royal Commissioners or by departmental committees; and their jurisdiction may be exercised by virtue of the simple prerogative of the Crown or by this together with the sanction of legislation.[1] Parliamentary investigations are generally conducted by means of "select" committees of one of the Houses of Parliament, occasionally by joint committees of both Houses, and, in rare circumstances, by a mixed political "conference" to which nonmembers of Parliament may be summoned.

Of these various organs of inquiry Royal Commissions are unquestionably the most ancient and the most dignified. But like so many other institutions of considerable antiquity, their origins are lost in hazy mists of the incompletely recorded past. The roots from which the Royal Commission procedure has

[1] When there is the additional statutory foundation, the commission is usually called a Statutory Commission; a departmental committee under similar circumstances is usually styled an Advisory Committee.

sprung are hidden in the many undifferentiated branches of the early royal administrations. Accordingly, the following account of their source and growth is intended not as a definitive or complete history but rather as a brief and suggestive explanation of the rise of this institution.

Royal Commissions are appointed by the Crown either by virtue of the prerogative or by authority of an act of Parliament; they depend, therefore, upon simple royal warrant or upon royal warrant issued in pursuance of parliamentary permission or instruction. In consequence of this legal basis, the history of Royal Commissions is closely interwoven with the constitutional struggles which have centered about the royal prerogative, and their development is closely connected with the attempts made at various periods to restrict royal action to certain definite and legalized modes of procedure. From Angevin days, numerous efforts have been made either to abolish Royal Commissions completely or to confine their use to certain types and purposes already recognized or specially admitted by statute. In the largest aspect of the subject, then, Royal Commissions have prospered or declined with the fluctuations of the supremacy of the Crown.

Broadly it may be said that the development of Royal Commissions falls into the five major stages which coincide with chief periods of English constitutional history: (1) the later Middle Ages; (2) the Tudor and early Stuart era; (3) Hanoverian England; (4) the nineteenth century; and (5) the present day. In the first period (1066–1485) Royal Commissions had their origin and experienced the first restrictions. In the second period (1485–1689) they underwent a wide extension, which culminated in their abolition. The third stage (1689–1800) was one in which they were either in complete abeyance or were overshadowed by other parliamentary organs. Then, in the nineteenth century, and particularly under Queen Victoria, Royal Commissions not only came into renewed vigor but attained their most significant development. It may be affirmed that in the present stage, commencing with 1914, they linger on as occasional agencies of inquiry, although they are to a large extent displaced or superseded, but not overshadowed, by new committees and conferences. The present chapter will be confined to the story of the rise and growth of Royal Commissions to the end of the seventeenth century.

FIRST STAGE AND EARLY OPPOSITION

Although Royal Commissions are now often regarded as primarily organs for the preliminary consideration of legislative policy on important social and economic problems, the origins of this form of investigation have no connection with Parliament. As the name implies, Royal Commissions owe their foundation to an exercise of the royal prerogative. The source of their existence is to be found in the generally assumed right of the Crown to appoint officials to perform duties temporarily or permanently on behalf of the King. In this sense the members of the Royal Commissions share their status with all other Royal Commissioners, i.e., with those officers whose authority is derived from appointment under royal seal, such as the officers of the army, colonial governors, justices of the peace, judges, and sheriffs.[2] In the widest meaning of the term, then, Royal Commissioners are those appointees of the Crown whose functions are specified in the formal document which authorizes their acting for certain purposes in the name of the Crown. It will be evident that this monograph is concerned not with all royally commissioned officials but only with such of them as are primarily devoted to investigative purposes. Administrative and judicial commissions are therefore beyond the scope of the discussion, except in so far as the one is connected in origin or development with the other; and the moment that temporary commissions of inquiry turn into permanent bodies—as often happens, and is in fact the tendency—our interest in them ceases.

In the earliest stages of royal administration there was little differentiation of function; the various duties now assigned to separate officials were not carefully distinguished. The highest officers of state were, of course, at Westminster (earlier at Winchester) and formed in varying degrees the court of the King, *curia regis,* the core of the royal council. Locally throughout the kingdom, royal authority was bestowed upon a somewhat irregular hierarchy of officials, such as the sheriffs and the royal bailiffs. In addition to these more or less permanent officials, special Commissioners were occasionally appointed for inspectional and investigative purposes. The most

[2] On the various types of appointment by letters patent under the different seals, *vide* W. R. Anson, *Law and Custom of the Constitution,* (4th ed., 1935) Vol. II, Part I, pp. 48–52, 65, 220–22.

noteworthy case is that of the Domesday Book, which was compiled between 1080 and 1086 by Royal Commissioners (variously styled barons, justices, *legati,* and *missi*) who were sent by William I into every county to ascertain the ownership of each estate of land and its value for taxation. In some places the entire county was summoned by these Commissioners, though usually the information was secured from a sworn jury from each hundred within the county. The result of their labors was the compilation of a mass of information respecting landholding, cultivation, and population of the manors throughout England at the date of the Conquest and of the survey. The Domesday survey may therefore be regarded as the result of the first Royal Commission of Inquiry.

It has been doubted whether the practice of sending special Commissioners into the several shires continued during the rest of the Norman period. At any rate it was not until the reign of Henry I that itinerant justices were to be found, and then only spasmodically. The chief purposes for which they were used were undoubtedly the maintenance of royal justice and the enforcement of those rights in which the King had a financial interest. By 1118 the subjects of inquiry by the justices had become sufficiently definite to be enumerated in the *Leges Henrici* as the usual "pleas of the crown." Yet despite the predominance of their judicial and financial duties, the itinerant justices still performed purely informational services. The typical Norman-Angevin machinery of the "inquest" by sworn juries, which was essentially a fact-finding process for both administrative and judicial purposes and which was taken over or adapted by the itinerant justices, is in consequence closely related to the early procedure of inquiry.

During the reign of Henry II the difficulties which arose from the appointment of local magnates as Commissioners and the recurrent trouble necessitated by the special commissioning of the numerous justices may well have been contributory reasons for the reform of this haphazard process by means of the Henrician reorganization. At some time about 1166 the itineraries of professional judges were organized into circuits and the scope of their duties was regularized and co-ordinated with the other judicial reforms for which Henry II is famed. To a large degree the justices in eyre were chiefly concerned with the preservation of royal rights, the conduct of criminal trials, and the adjudication of private causes in the new possessory assizes. At times, however, the itinerant justices were engaged in other and larger tasks. There was for instance the noted Inquest of Sheriffs in 1176, by which special panels of justices were commissioned to inquire into the abuses and injustices which were attributed to sheriffs and local officials whose accounts they were to inspect and audit. As in the Domesday inquest, the barons named as Royal Commissioners took evidence under oath from the baronage and freeholders of the county respecting the receipts of the sheriffs, bishops, and all other royal officials connected with the exchequer or royal domain.

During these early centuries the line between royal justice and other administrative and fiscal functions of the Government was only just beginning to emerge.

The entire scheme of governmental machinery was still in an embryonic form, and the differentiation between various departments was still only just becoming apparent. Once commissioners or itinerant justices were introduced as a mechanism for supervision of local administration of justice and royal rights, it was an obvious and convenient policy for the central authorities to add additional articles to their commissions and extend their functions on occasion beyond the customary tasks of gaol delivery (oyer and terminer), possessory assizes, and pleas of the Crown.

The close connection between the use of commissioners for justice, administration, inquiry, and legislation is further demonstrated by the reign of Henry II. The regularization of circuits was accomplished by the Assize of Clarendon (1166) and was revised by the Assize of Northampton (1176), both of which statutes determined the nature and purposes of the itinerant judicial process. Then, as the central control over the whole land was attained, the justices were utilized (e.g., in 1173) to supervise the destruction of castles, to prevent the sale of ships and timber out of the kingdom, to assess tallages, and to enroll promises to pay for special privileges (*fines* and *conventiones*). Special justices were commissioned for the Assize of Arms (1181), for the forest law and its enforcement (Assize of Woodstock, 1184), and for the purpose (1194) of making an extraordinary inquiry into the fiscal rights of the King.

A century later, under the energetic hand of Edward I, a further enlargement of specially commissioned itinerant justices implemented the tightening of central control over local justice and the reform of landholding. At the commencement of Edward's reign, the inquest into the local liberties and franchises of the barons resulted in the second great survey of the kingdom in the "Hundred Rolls," and led to the further statutory inquiry by the Commissioners through *quo warranto* proceedings into the judicial jurisdiction held by local magnates (Statute of Gloucester, 1278). In a similar fashion the other legal reforms of the reign were administered by the justices in eyre or by special Commissioners, examples being the extension of the common law to Wales (1284), the Mortmain regulations for the church lands (1279), mercantile law (*de mercatoribus,* 1283), and the new police and arms regulations of the Statute of Winchester (1285).

Thus it may be seen that long before the establishment of Parliament or of modern legislative procedure Royal Commissions had become a feature of English administration. To a large extent the growth of this type of investigation proceeded *pari passu* with the development of royal justice and administration. For a long period the terminology was not differentiated, and it is difficult to determine at what date the Inquest into local crimes, property rights, and misconduct by royal agents for the purpose of punishment or retribution became distinct from the Inquiry which was intended to precede relief from injustice or to serve as the basis for legislation. It is the close connection of early justice, revenue, and administration, and the common origin of the inquest and inquiry which has produced the somewhat incoherent nomenclature of modern times by which investigators, judges, and permanent administrators are all designated Royal Commissioners.[3]

Needless to say, the extension of centralization by Royal Commissioners of whatever type was not accomplished without bitter opposition from the local magnates. Magna Carta was drafted largely for the purpose of reducing the expanding jurisdiction of the King. Throughout the document it is apparent that the barons were concerned with the restriction of royal functions and institutions to such definite and ancient forms as could not be challenged. In particular there was a great fear of the authority of new royal appointees, and in numerous articles there is insistence that local juries should accompany royal inquisition. In this most famous document there is also to be found what may be regarded as the first nonroyal inquiry: Twelve sworn knights were to be elected by the honest men of each shire to inquire immediately into the bad customs concerning forests and foresters, and sheriffs and their servants, so that these customs might be destroyed forever after the King or his justiciar had been notified.

Magna Carta was not completely successful in reducing royal powers, as its frequent confirmations by Henry III and Edward I reveal. But, in the main, it created a presumption against the legality of any

[3] All three have to "inquire" into the facts; but a Commission of Inquiry "inquires" in order to report; a judicial commission authorizes the judge to "hear and determine" the cases inquired into; and the administrative body often inquires and reports but is primarily concerned with the enforcement of regulations either in pursuance of statutory provision or in conformity with the Crown's discretion. The line between inquiry for report and inquiry for adjudication is quite definite today, but the distinction between inquiry for administration and inquiry for adjudication gives rise to serious controversy. There is an increasing number of treatises upon this problem of administrative law.

new judicial or administrative agencies. Moreover, the rise of Parliament at the close of the thirteenth century seemed to indicate that the need for the old Commissions of Inquiry was being outgrown. The development of the representative principle in the House of Commons, by which typical knights, burgesses, and freeholders were brought to Westminster as the "Great Inquest into the State of the Nation," could be interpreted as superseding the special inquests ordered by the monarch. That such a view was vaguely felt at the time may be inferred from the fact that when the justices of the peace—a new group of judicial officers acting without jury—were commissioned by Edward III, this action was preceded by statutory approval. Each extension of the justices' multitudinous duties during the next three centuries was similarly authorized by parliamentary enactment.

Nevertheless, despite the recognition of Parliament as the Grand Inquest of the Nation, the appointment of special commissions did not entirely cease. Inquisition, with or without the check of the twelve lawful men of the shire or hundred, was still utilized by the Crown for numerous purposes extending from determination of local and private rights to extraordinary criminal investigations. In addition to the assessment of unusual taxes, the recruitment of armies (commissions of array), and the suppression of riots and disorder in the lawless period of "livery and maintenance," special inquiries were used to check overzealous officials and to determine numerous questions of fact important to the Crown. The continued use of special commissioners produced a series of attempts on the part of several Parliaments under the first three Edwards to place a definite prohibition upon these undesirable commissions. Thus in 1344 the House of Commons demanded the abolition of all "novelle Enquerez," and Edward III assented ("les Commissions des novelle Enquerez cessent de tut"), except for the older processes before the justices.[4] Shortly after this a more sweeping enactment not only specified certain notorious commissions but declared that these and all commissions of like nature were wholly and entirely contrary to the laws and statutes of the realm.[5]

It was intended, apparently, not to abolish entirely the inquiring function of the Crown but merely to restrict its use to cases sanctioned by the House of Commons. Thus in 1325 the Commons had petitioned Edward II for investigation into the violation of the forest charter by "les Ministres de la Foreste," and this was granted by the commissioning of high clergy and officials for the purpose.[6] Similarly in 1341 another petition was accepted for inquiry into the conduct of certain royal officers and the fines they had levied.[7] Royal Commissions, then, still continued to

[4] 2 *Rotuli Parliamentorum,* pp. 148–49.

[5] 34 Edward III, c. i: "All general inquiries before this time granted within any signories, for the mischiefs and oppressions which have been done to the people by such inquiries, shall cease utterly and be repealed." This is still upon the statute book. *The Consolidated Index of Statutes* summarizes it as "general commissions of inquiry abolished." But it seems clear that this is too broad an interpretation. These early statutes were all directed against special types of commission and against commissions which possessed judicial and administrative functions as well as those of inquiry. Cf. W. H. Moore, "Executive Commissions of Inquiry," *Columbia Law Review,* XIII (1913), 501–23.

[6] 1 *Rot. Parl.,* p. 430.

[7] 2 *Rot. Parl.,* p. 129. The *Rolls* contain numerous other cases of this kind. *Cf.* Index, Vol. VII, under "Commissions," "Commissioners," "Inquest," "Inquiry."

be appointed when they were sanctioned by statute, when their duties were in accord with the accustomed law of the land, or when they were granted in response to a petition of the Grand Inquest of the Nation; but there was definite resistance to the appointment of commissions with new and extended powers not contemplated by the rather vague law of the land.

EXTENSIVE USE BY THE TUDORS

A second stage in the development of Royal Commissions opened with the accession of Henry VII. The Tudor and Stuart periods are characterized by the enlargement of royal functions; as an accompaniment of this there was an increased use of commissions for inquisitional as well as for semijudicial and administrative purposes. Many historians have attempted to distinguish between the Tudor and Stuart despotisms by affirming that the former was legalized, while the latter was contrary to law.[8] But this judgment comes chiefly from accepting contemporary opinion. Fundamentally, both Tudor and Stuart governments rested on the same foundations; but, whereas Tudor absolutism was unchallenged, Stuart absolutism was resisted and finally overthrown.

In a very real sense the first Tudor monarch held his place on the English throne by parliamentary authority. Yet during the ensuing century, although parliamentary approval was sought for certain essen-

[8] Thus Sir John A. R. Marriott writes: "But if the Tudors were dictators, they were almost invariably careful to clothe their dictatorship with the forms of law" (*The Crisis of English Liberty* [1930], p. 29). It is surprising, that in a book professing to study the encroachments of the Stuarts upon common law and Parliament in the light of the recent discussions of administrative law this author should have neglected completely the consideration of Commissions at that period.

tial pieces of legislation, the monarch regarded the Parliament as a tool for the enforcement of royal will; and Parliaments proved in fact to be decidedly subservient bodies. The Houses were rarely summoned, and when they were assembled it was for little more than to approve policies already determined upon.

The characteristic agencies of Tudor government were the Privy Council and Royal Commissions.[9] During the hundred and fifty years which follow 1485 the most significant features of royal administration are to be found in the enlargement of central authority by the following methods: Privy Council ordinance and proclamation; special political and criminal justice in the Star Chamber; religious control by the High Commission; and the development of numerous other organs for administration, such as the Council of the North, the Council of Wales, and the Court of Castle Chamber. Alongside these more or less permanent institutions were the countless special commissions which either were constituted as an outgrowth of the bodies mentioned or were created *de novo*. Examples are numerous. In 1539 a Commission was sent to Calais to examine the proceedings of Lord Lisle. In 1550 another Commission was sent by Edward VI to

[9] No one ever doubted the power of the Council to inquire into matters affecting the Government and the State. As early as 1553 the Council had been divided into five committees, each of which pursued official inquiries when necessary. In addition to these committees, "the Council found another method of informing itself of specific matters and of taking steps to deal with the rapidly changing conditions, viz. by means of Commissions of Inquiry which are analogous to the Royal Commissions of today. Members of these Commissions were not always Privy Councillors, but rather were men who had a particular knowledge of the business at hand. F. J. Port, *Administrative Law* (1929), pp. 41–42. It is submitted that these Commissions of Inquiry were in most cases, if not in all, true Royal Commissions.

partition the "debatable lands" of the northern border.[10] And as an example of the participation of the Council in inquiry may be cited the questioning of Lady Arabella Stuart (in the line of royal succession) respecting her marriage to a son of the Earl of Hertford.[11]

It is unnecessary to enter here into the causes which permitted the sudden extension of royal authority. The changing economic and social conditions which followed the Black Death, the reduction of the powers of the barons, and the rise of prices caused by the influx of gold after the discovery of America were sound reasons for the increase of national control by Parliament. But it is evident that Parliament was no longer a thoroughly representative body. The restriction of the county franchise in 1430 to the forty-shilling freeholders removed from influence the yeomanry and lesser landholders. Accordingly, when the profitable woolen industry encouraged the increase of sheepwalks and the enclosure of common lands no voice was raised in Parliament to explain the disastrous effects these changes were producing upon the laboring classes. Yet the consequences could not be neglected; depopulation of the country and the growth of unrest provided prob-

[10] "This commission," remarks Lord Eustace Percy, "is worthy of notice as it illustrates in a remarkable way how little faith the Tudor Council put in the advice of the 'man on the spot.' The Councillors direct that it were best to have the devision [*sic*] agreed upon by Commissioners not being upon the place, for that they shall on both parts be impeached with the disordered affections of the people there" (*The Privy Council under the Tudors* [1907], p. 36 n.).

[11] Countess of Shrewsbury's Case, 1612. *Vide* J. Baldwin, *The King's Council in England during the Middle Ages* (1903), p. 300. Her refusal to answer was agreed to be a high contempt of the King; but it was determined that this was a question for the Star Chamber rather than for a committee of the Privy Council.

lems which had to be faced by the Government no matter how easily they might be disregarded by the gentry.

The type of inquiry which resulted from the social changes is best observed in the most famous of all the early Tudor bodies, the Commission on Enclosures of 1517. This inquiry—which has frequently, but erroneously, been regarded as one of the first Royal Commissions[12]—was distinctively of the modern type, though its secondary historic title as the "Domesday Book of Enclosures" indicates that its relation to the first Domesday Book was clearly perceived. The warrants of appointment named a number of the principal noblemen and gentlemen of the counties for the purpose of study of this social problem with a view to government action.[13] After the report by the Commissioners the Government took such action against the landlords "as struck terror among them."[14] Not only was no time lost by the Government in following up the reports of the Commission with active measures but fresh commissions were issued in the years following, both to supply comple-

[12] W. Ashley, *An Introduction to English Economic History and Theory* (1910), II, 283. Sir William Ashley's dictum has been relied upon by several later writers, including H. F. Gosnell, "British Royal Commissions of Enquiry," *Political Science Quarterly*, XLIX (1934), 84 n.

[13] *Vide* I. S. Leadam (ed.), *The Domesday Book of Enclosures, 1517–18* (Royal Historical Society, 1897). For the controversial aspects, cf. "The Inquisitions of Depopulation in 1517 and the Domesday of Enclosures," *Transactions of the Royal Historical Society*, New Series, XIV (1900), 231 ff.

[14] J. Macy, *The English Constitution* (1906), p. 222. *The Domesday Book of Enclosures* describes the suits which were begun on the part of the Crown for half the profits. Later it was decreed that a fine of £100 would be imposed on those failing to "pull down and lay abroad all enclosures and ditches made since the I Henry VII" unless evidence showed that the enclosure was more beneficial to the Commonwealth than the pulling down thereof. *Ibid.*, I, 10–11.

mentary evidence and to return cases previously overlooked.[15] Legislation frequently followed the reports with the avowed object of preventing "depopulation" of the countryside and the withdrawal of land from cultivation.

"From this time," comments Sir William Ashley, "the idea of a royal commission was never absent from the mind of politicians."[16] The device was utilized for more limited investigations, as in the inquiry into the grievances of the East Anglia textile workers in 1630. In another sphere, too, Commissions were used in the modern fashion. Consolidation of the statutes of the realm had been suggested by Sir Nicholas Bacon, Lord-Keeper under Elizabeth, but it was not until James I referred to the confusion of laws by "divers cross and cuffing statutes"[17] that a Royal Commission was issued for the purpose of reducing the chaos of the statute book to order. That the labors of the Commissioners resulted in nothing more than a manuscript, now preserved in the British Museum,

[15] E.g., 1518, 1519, 1548–49, 1566, 1607, 1632, 1636. Cf. A. E. Bland, P. A. Brown, and R. H. Tawney, *English Economic History: Select Documents* (1921), pp. 262–64.

[16] Ashley, *op. cit.*, II, 283. That it might become a popular safety valve by virtue of the belief that all ills could be cured by a Commission appears from Sir William Forrest's *Pleasant Poesye of Princelie Practice*, written in 1548. After suggesting that rents be reduced to the level of forty years before, the poem proceeds to suggest a Commission to value all farms:

"In which youre highnes this ordre maye take, discreit men of youre counsell too assigne that wilbee corrupted for no mannys sake: and theye withe helpe their endever tenclyne, over youre Royalme wheare this is owte of lyne. Growndis and ffermys to peruse and surveye: Rentis to reforme that bee owte of the weye. And as their Wisdoms (with Conscience) shall see, (with soyle consydered, barrayne or fertyle) the owners (by them) ordered to bee their Rentis tabute, enhaunced so longe while. Pryvate Commodye to put to exile, ratynge the same indifferentlie so; the ffermers to lyne and by them oother moe." Extract in appendix to S. J. Herrtage (ed.), *England in the Reign of King Henry the Eighth* (1878), Part I, "Starkey's Life and Letters."

[17] C. Ilbert, *The Mechanics of Law-Making* (1914), p. 26.

reveals that nineteenth-century Commissions are not the only ones which have proved abortive.

It is, however, in the realm of religion that the widest extension of the Commission practice was evoked in the late Tudor and early Stuart times.[18] The breach with the Church of Rome not only necessitated a very considerable reorganization and redistribution of Church properties but shortly occasioned a profound adaptation of ceremony and doctrine to standardize the nature and degree of religious reformation in England. When the change from a Roman to an Anglican Church was instituted it was accomplished by parliamentary authority; yet, while vesting in the King the headship of the Church, it permitted royal supremacy to be exercised by royal delegation of power, i.e., by Royal Commission. Scores of Commissions were accordingly set up in the course of the century after 1530. In 1533, for instance, Henry VIII had assumed the task of rooting out heresy, a function formerly undertaken either by the ecclesiastical courts or by special commission from the Pope or his legate (as in 1521 when Wolsey had delegated to the bishops his legatine power for the purpose of searching for heretical books). Then, as the separation from Rome took an active form, there were Commissions for first fruits (1535 and 1536), and for the valuation of benefices (1535), as well as for divorces and for the collection of lead, plate, and ornaments from the churches and chantries (1551–52).

The most important of all ecclesiastical bodies was

[18] For the information in the next few pages chief reliance has been placed upon R. G. Usher, *The Rise and Fall of the High Commission* (1913).

a Commission (on which sat clerics and laymen, lawyers and privy councillors) established for the purpose of exercising the wide royal powers of ecclesiastical discipline. This Commission was first created in 1535 by Thomas Cromwell, to whom Henry had transferred the full plenitude of his powers over the Church; and, though the original document has been lost, it seems to have been the antecedent of the later High Commission. Among the first tasks of the Commission was the visitation of the monasteries and convents with an eye to their suppression. Other Commissions were also set up by Cromwell, and their field of action was shortly extended to the suppression of Anabaptists. After the death of Henry VIII the Edwardian reforms were enforced by another High Commission (1549). At Mary's succession to the throne the same organ seems to have been the chief agency for restoring Catholic doctrine and ceremony in the Church.

The return of the monarchy to a Protestant foundation with the accession of Elizabeth has always been regarded as the source from which the historic High Commission sprang. That this is not the case has already been indicated; but that it was believed to be so may have arisen from loss of the Henrician Commission and from the continuous life that the High Commission now gained, for the Elizabethan Church settlement was the only permanent establishment of the century. Yet the Commission was not new, and, oddly enough, two members of Mary's Catholic Commission sat upon the new one appointed by Elizabeth in 1659.

The fact that the Elizabethan High Commission

soon resolved itself into a court and into a permanent administrative agency—a development similar to that which had overtaken circuit judges and justices of the peace—must not blind us to the early possibilities of this Commission. Elizabeth apparently had in mind more than the creation of a body to do for religion what Chancery and the Star Chamber had done for the inequitable phases of common law and criminal administration. She had intended to have the Commission serve as an advisory body for the determination of ritual, doctrine, vestments, and discipline in the new establishment. This purpose was contemplated by the Act of Supremacy of 1559 (section viii);[19] and in 1561, in accordance with this intention, the Queen in addressing the Commissioners required four of them to revise the Scripture lessons and the calendar, to consider the decay of churches, and to see that "one maner be used" in the cathedral and parish churches. In conformity with this order, although the Commissioners are not known to be responsible for the Thirty-Nine Articles, they did attempt to redraft the catechism and to examine all clergymen. They also endorsed Bishop Jewel's famous *Apology* for the new Church settlement.

DEFINITE RESTRICTION IN THE SEVENTEENTH CENTURY

That the High Commission finally degenerated into a court for the determination of ecclesiastical causes and for the maintenance of discipline within the establishment was an unexpected development which ultimately proved its undoing. Not only was its juris-

[19] Usher, *op. cit.*, p. 52, cites the Act of Uniformity, section xiii; but this is clearly an error.

diction challenged by the common-law judges under James I, as in the case of Prohibitions (1607),[20] but at the same time, since it was without statutory authority as a court, the High Commission became one of the chief objects of the Puritans' hostility. Supported as it was by legal opinion, the Puritan opposition, when it gained control of Parliament, proceeded to abolish not only this supposedly illegal body but also many other instruments of Stuart tyranny. The story of this attack on Stuart misgovernment is well known and needs no recapitulation. The results of it were the extinction of the royal power to make new law by ordinance (the case of Proclamations, 1610),[21] the cancellation of commissions granting persons or corporate bodies industrial or commercial monopolies (Act against Monopolies, 1624), and the prohibition of commissions for enforcement of martial law (Petition of Rights, 1628),[22] as well as the abolition of the High Commission, the Star Chamber, and four other courts named in the acts of 1641.[23] The Grand Remonstrance of 1641 went further. In the unending catalogue of governmental injustices there were named the Commissions "for examining

[20] 12 *Coke's Reports*, p. 63. [21] *Ibid.*, p. 74.

[22] The provision in the Petition of Rights has often been relied upon for the complete prohibition of all Royal Commissions; but the phrasing, "which commissions, and all other of like nature, are wholly and directly contrary to the said laws and statutes of this realm" (section ix), clearly refers to the specific commissioners for the army, in the same way that the earlier portion of the Petition refers to commissioners appointed to collect benevolences and forced loans.

[23] Here again it is true that the chief objection was to the power of these Commissions and courts to try and punish individuals without juries and regardless of the usual forms of common-law procedure. The same objection was taken to the court of Chancery, which however escaped abolition, though it was named in the Grand Remonstrance (section 43), along with the Exchequer, the Court of Wards, "and other English Courts," as having exceeded its jurisdiction.

the excess of fees" (section 49), and the Commission turning convocation into a synod, "in which, by an unheard-of presumption, they made canon . . . ." and "imposed a new oath upon divers of His Majesty's subjects" (sections 85, 86).

The victory of the parliamentary party in the civil wars preceding the execution of Charles I left no doubt that Royal Commissions which put the subject on oath, sought to punish by fine or imprisonment, or attempted the enforcement of new or old laws in any other than the historic forms of laws were illegal unless they had definite statutory foundation. This did not mean that no Royal Commissions might be issued, but it did necessitate parliamentary approval for their appointment. It was in accordance with this rule that the second statute of James I (1604) had, at an earlier date, named Commissioners to "treat and consult with" certain Scottish Commissioners "concerning such an union of the said realms of England and Scotland," the results of which "doings and proceedings" were to be written "that thereupon such further proceedings may be had as by both the said parliaments shall be thought fit and necessary for the weal and common good of both the said realms." Even the Long Parliament, which swept aside scores of prerogative Royal Commissions, provided for inquiry into the metes and bounds of the forests by "commissions under the Great Seal of England."[24]

At the close of this second period, the period in

[24] 16 Charles I, c. 16 (1641). Yet it must be noted that Commissioners were to be nominated by the Houses of Parliament, and were to "enquire of and find out by inquests of good and lawful men upon oath, and by

which they had attained their greatest development of use and function, we find Royal Commissions left in what appears an anomalous position. All the most important and significant Commissions had been abolished in the course of the struggles which reduced the active exercise of the powers of the Crown. Moreover, the opinion of the greatest jurist of these centuries was expressed against their legality in no uncertain terms.[25] Yet no formal declaration can properly be said to assert in undeniable terms that all Royal Commissions were illegal. The cases that are relied upon for this purpose are unsatisfactory either as to reporting or as to pertinence.[26] The unpopularity into which Royal Commissions had fallen came

the oaths of witnesses to be produced at the said inquests, and by all other lawful means" (section vi).

In this connection it is interesting to note that the Grand Remonstrance contemplated the establishment of a religious "conference" comparable to those which have sat in recent years upon electoral reform, the second chamber, and a united Ireland. The Westminster Assembly of Divines was foreshadowed by section 185 of the Grand Remonstrance: "And the better to effect the intended reformation [in religion], we desire that there may be a general synod of the most grave, pious, learned and judicious divines of this island: assisted with some from foreign parts, professing the same religion with us, who may consider of all things necessary for the peace and good government of the Church, and represent the results of their consultations unto the Parliament, to be there allowed of and confirmed, and receive the stamp of authority, thereby to find passage and obedience throughout the kingdom."

[25] In numerous places Sir Edward Coke declared against Royal Commissions: 2 *Institutes*, pp. 4, 78, and 165; 4 *Inst.*, pp. 163, 245, and 324. He had also been one of the prime movers for the Petition of Right.

[26] E.g., Case of Commissions of Inquiry, reported by Coke (12 *Reports*, p. 31) as of 1603, was not printed until 1656; and though Coke therein declared against the legality of the Commission to inquire into the depopulation of houses, etc.—"for by this a man may be unjustly accused by perjury, and he shall not have remedy"—such Commissions did continue to investigate enclosures. So Whitelocke's Case (2 *Howard's State Trials*, p. 768), in which Coke advised Sir Robert Mansel, treasurer of the Navy, that a Royal Commission to inquire into the abuses of the Navy was illegal, did not result in a clear-cut decision by the Star Chamber before which the case came. Bacon, it may be remarked, advised that the Commission was legal, although admitting that some Commissions (those inquiring into private matters) were illegal.

chiefly from the exercise of unlawful jurisdiction of an administrative and judicial type. Actually there was little objection to inquiry pure and simple, although the penetrating mind of Coke had perceived the possibility of unrestrained libel and false accusation which this might and did engender. Such a danger, however, is inseparable from any form of inquiry, royal or parliamentary, as was demonstrated by the famous *Stockdale* vs. *Hansard* case in 1839.[27]

One may conclude, then, by saying that, though Commissions of Inquiry were not clearly abolished, as were many other types of commission for administration and judication, such an odor of unconstitutionality was attached to all Royal Commissions not having parliamentary authority that the Crown would hesitate in the future to incur popular displeasure by utilizing them when Crown and Parliament were not in close political harmony.

IN ABEYANCE DURING THE EIGHTEENTH CENTURY

The third stage in the history of Royal Commissions is one of decay and insignificance. The restriction of royal authority to legal and parliamentary forms, which was the general consequence of the Revolution of 1688, removed the foundations upon which Royal Commissions had been based. It was not so much the change of law that mattered, for this was not very great; the essential thing was that the political center of gravity had moved from the Crown

[27] In this case Stockdale sued Hansard as the parliamentary publisher of a report of the inspector of prisons which contained libelous statements respecting the plaintiff. Judgment was given for Stockdale (3 *State Trials*, New Series, pp. 723 ff.). In consequence of this decision a statutory protection was accorded to privileged papers of the Houses of Parliament (3 & 4 Victoria, c. 9).

to Parliament. When the Restoration of 1660 had taken place, no legal change whatsoever, it may be said, had occurred in the status of the monarchy. Not even after the suspension of parliamentary government by Charles II and later by his brother, James II, was there any very decided legal transformation. The Bill of Rights (1689), which, with the Mutiny Act (1689) and the Habeas Corpus Act (1679), was the chief change so far as this matter of Royal Commissions is concerned, contained no general provisions. The Habeas Corpus Act was directed to restraining arbitrary arrest; the Mutiny Act placed courts martial under parliamentary sanction for limited periods only, and the Bill of Rights merely repeated the former denunciation of the Ecclesiastical Commission ("and all other commissions and courts of like nature").[28]

The rule was thenceforth firmly established: Royal Commissions for administrative and judicial purposes were definitely illegal if they sought to enforce new ordinances; and all Commissions, whether for administration or for inquiry, were illegal if they were to be a charge on the subject or were not supported by parliamentary appropriation. It was thus possible for Blackstone in the middle of the eighteenth century to repeat almost word for word the statements of Coke.[29]

[28] On his return in 1660 Charles II had appointed a Commission of bishops and clergymen to revise the prayer book; but instead of attempting to enforce the decisions of this body, as had been done by James I and Charles I, the revision was given statutory approval by the Act of Uniformity (1662). James II made the serious mistake of establishing a court for ecclesiastical affairs on the lines of the early High Commission, and it was this return to a royal enforcement which led to the provision of the Bill of Rights.

[29] *Commentaries*, Bk. I, chap. 7. Blackstone's ground was that the

Yet this in itself does not completely explain the decline of Royal Commissions in the Hanoverian period. The Revolution settlement only made more certain the previous situation and ended the use of illegal Commissions. The right of the Crown to conduct simple inquiries was never abolished, and the use of Commissions with parliamentary approval still remained. Moreover, as the chief change in the constitutional system consisted in the introduction of a harmonious relation between Crown and Parliament, it might be thought that Royal Commissions could be more regularly utilized. That such was not the case was the result of three forces.

In the first place, the recollection of the pernicious effects of Royal Commissions carried with it such memories of Stuart tyranny that few ministers of the Crown could be found to assume responsibility for using the instruments of this hated and feared despotism. When Commissions were required, these ministers, possessing normally sufficient influence within the Houses of Parliament, did secure statutory confirmation for the inquiry. But such occasions were rare. One of them is noteworthy. In 1706 the scheme for the union of the Parliaments of England and Scotland was planned by Commissions appointed for both countries, and the resultant articles ("with additions and explanations") were later passed in both Parliaments. So occasionally in other cases special inquiries were entered into with statutory endorsement.[30]

King cannot create new offices with new fees annexed to them (citing Coke, 2 *Inst.*, 533); but he had no objection to Royal Commissions which were unpaid or were supported by parliamentary funds or statutes.

[30] A Commission was suggested in 1689 when the Earl of Nottingham

A second reason for the decline of Royal Commissions is to be found in the development of a new and more typical parliamentary agency, the committee. The use of committees by the two Houses goes back to the fourteenth century. Originally petitions presented to the House of Commons were dealt with in the first place by receivers and triers appointed by the King (and such sinecure appointments lasted long into the nineteenth century); but late in the fourteenth century certain petitions were referred to committees; e.g., in 1399 petitions from several boroughs asking for relief from taxes were sent to committees of the House of Lords.[31]

By the close of the sixteenth century the procedure of setting up "select" committees was firmly established, and as the Stuart period opened perhaps the most noted of these was the Committee on Grievances. Indeed the power which could be secured by the House of Commons through the use of committees was perhaps the chief discovery of the parliamentary opposition.[32] At any rate, during the struggle against Charles I innumerable committees were set up by the Puritan leaders of Parliament. The list of commit-

introduced a bill to authorize a Commission appointed by the King to discuss with the dissenters the points of difference between them and the Church. The bill met bitter opposition for political reasons; and some members of the House of Lords entered a "protest," not against a Commission, but against the exclusion of laymen from the proposed Commission, and also because it might be a device "to elude repeated promises . . . . when the providing for it is taken out of the ordinary course of parliament." *Protests of the Lords* (T. Rogers, ed.) I, 74–76.

In 1717 and 1719 Royal Commissions were appointed to inquire into the estates of recusants.

[31] 3 *Rot. Parl.*, p. 447. Committees were already used for financial purposes, e.g., to collect the tallage voted in 1337, and again in 1340 to audit accounts. 2 *Rot. Parl.*, p. 114.

[32] W. Notestein, "Winning of the Initiative by the House of Commons," *Proceedings of the British Academy*, XI (1924–25), 125–75.

tees, for example, upon which Pym served in the first three Parliaments of the reign is a record of the progress of the disputes.[33] The Civil War was undertaken, on the parliamentary side, by means of committee government.

After the Revolution of 1688 the select-committee procedure continued as the characteristic parliamentary device for inquiry.[34] But it was no longer the weapon of a hostile House of Commons, as it had been formerly. From the moment that royal ministers held office by virtue of their political influence in Parliament, it was clear that the select committees set up by the parliamentary majority would be dominated by the Cabinet members who controlled that majority. The Crown, therefore, through its ministers, had in the committee system an effective procedure for inquiry purposes. Hundreds of select committees were set up during the eighteenth century for the purpose of considering both public and private legislation, the enclosure of common lands, administrative questions, the determination of disputed elections, etc. Perhaps the most noted parliamentary inquiry during the century was the secret committee of twenty-one members appointed after Walpole's resignation in 1742 to investigate his conduct during the

[33] The forty or more appointments per session are enumerated in C. E. Wade, *John Pym* (1912), Appendices II–VI.

[34] The view given currency by Hallam, that parliamentary inquiries by select or special committees for the investigation of the conduct of the Government departments originated in 1689, is clearly false. In that year the mismanagement of the war in Ireland was investigated by a select committee (*Constitutional History of England,* III, 143). Although this judgment is quoted by Anson (*op. cit.,* ed. of 1922, II, 398) as sufficient authority, it is evident from what has already been said that committee inquiries had a much earlier origin. Parliamentary committees had been examining the accounts of the collectors of the revenue from as early as 1340.

preceding ten years[35]—a committee similar to one on which Walpole had sat at Bolingbroke's fall in 1715.

But there is a third explanation, quite apart from the disfavor with which Royal Commissions were viewed and the prominence of parliamentary committees, which restricted the use of Commissions. This is the lack of need for inquiry. After the constitutional position had been clarified by the "Glorious Revolution" and the church establishment had been assured, the victorious squirearchy felt little or no necessity for innovations or reform in the England they ruled. The eighteenth century was almost totally devoid of social or economic legislation of the reformist type. "Domestic legislation for the whole period of parliamentary conservatism was confined to small alterations of administrative law, to special or local enactments."[36] Although the century was one of the bitterest partisanship, the political rivalry was between opposing groups of families or of factional cliques with little or no relation to legislative policy. There was no consciousness of the need for inquiry into economic and social problems, because no changes were contemplated by the ruling powers. This was both a matter of complaint by later reformers and a ground of self-justification by the nineteenth-century Whigs. Bagehot[37] quotes Lord John

[35] It was expected that the findings of the committee would be the basis of impeachment proceedings, but the committee was unable to report as anticipated. This does not mean, however, that the popular accusations against Walpole were unfounded; it simply means that the committee did not desire to expose the Walpole system.

[36] J. Redlich, *The Procedure of the House of Commons* (1903), I, 66. He goes on: "The centre of gravity of the action of the House of Commons lay in the region of foreign and colonial policy and the financial measures rendered necessary by the decisions on such subjects."

[37] *Essays on Reform* (1883), p. 169.

Russell as remarking in the House of Commons that Lord Chatham, the most powerful Minister of the eighteenth century, had not passed a single legislative measure during his period of office. Instead of this the chief social and industrial legislation resulted from private interest and related chiefly to enclosure (by private act). Later in the century the most significant statutes were in the nature of repressive measures intended to suppress agitation and reformist tendencies. Yet when inquiries did become inevitable they were nearly always undertaken by committees of one House or the other.[38]

Nevertheless, despite the pre-eminence of committees in this period it must not be thought that Royal Commissions were completely nonexistent. In the midst of the committee system we find that Commissioners were repeatedly used for the partition of land, the supervision of enclosures, and such like matters.[39] Further, semiadministrative commissions for numerous governmental purposes continued from the previous period. Dr. Johnson's famous definition of the Excise as "a hateful tax levied upon commodities, and adjudged not by the common judges of property, but wretches hired by those to whom excise is paid" reveals how unpopular these administrative agencies were among the classes high above those for whom

[38] Prior to 1801 the most important reports of select committees were incorporated into the journals of the Houses of Parliament. A considerable number, however, were omitted; and in 1783 most of these were reprinted in four volumes, eleven more volumes being issued in 1803, with an index volume which also contained a list of the committee reports in the journals of the House of Commons (*Reports from the Committees of the House of Commons, 1715–1802,* 1803, 16 vols.). About one hundred and fifty reports which are not included in this re-publication are listed in *Third Report of the Select Committee on Committee Rooms and Printed Papers* (No. 516, 1825), Appendix 3.

[39] *Vide* F. Clifford, *A History of Private Bill Legislation* (1885), 2 vols.

Burns sang of the Exciseman. Even Blackstone in his lengthy glorification of the English constitution declaims against the increasing number of officials:

"The instruments of power are not perhaps so open and avowed as they formerly were, and therefore are the less liable to jealous and invidious reflections; but they are not the weaker upon that account. The entire collection and management of so vast a revenue, being placed in the hands of the crown, have given rise to such a multitude of new officers created by and removable at the royal pleasure that they have extended the influence of government to every corner of the nation. Witness the commissioners and the multitude of dependents on the customs in every port of the kingdom; the commissioners of excise, and their numerous subalterns, in every inland district; the post-masters, and their servants, planted in every town, and upon every public road; the commissioners of stamps, and their distributors, who are full as scattered and full as numerous; the officers of the salt duty, which though a species of excise and conducted in the same manner, are yet made a distinct corps from the ordinary managers of that revenue; the surveyors of houses and windows, the receivers of the land tax; the managers of lotteries; and the commissioner of hackney coaches, all which are either mediately or immediately appointed by the crown, and removable at pleasure without any reason assigned: these, it requires but little penetration to see, must give that power, on which they depend for subsistence, an influence most amazingly extensive."[40]

[40] W. Blackstone, *Commentaries on the Law of England,* Vol. I, Book 1, chap. 8.

CHAPTER III

THE NINETEENTH CENTURY, THE GREAT ERA OF COMMISSIONS

The questions of pauperism and poor-law administration, of crime and penal administration, of pestilence and sanitary legislation, and of the evils attendant on excessive manufacturing labour, are conspicuous instances of the effects of commissions of inquiry in reversing every main principle, and almost every assumed chief elementary fact, on which the general public, parliamentary committees, and leading statesmen, were prepared to legislate.—E. CHADWICK

IN ACTIVE EXISTENCE, 1800–1832

Royal Commissions of Inquiry came to their fullest development and most extensive use during the Victorian Age. While it might be expected that the prevalence of laissez-faire dogmas should be accompanied by an indifference on the part of the Government to the "state of the nation," the very reverse was the case. To a degree which was previously inconceivable, the guardians of the state became increasingly interested in investigating every phase of social life with a view to remedying the evils which were apparent. The original intention in these inquiries seems to have been the relief of industry and labor from the aggravating restrictions upon free capitalistic enterprise and for the reduction of the power of the existing vested interests; but the outcome of a series of inquiries into the operation of the older social restraints and of the new legislative proposals was, strangely enough, the discovery that new or additional restrictions upon the "liberated" industrial system were necessary. Countless inquiries were made during the course of the century into all phases of social life, both for the purpose of finding out the state of the nation in its economic and sociological processes and to discover what the nation was thinking. Thus, while the inquiries into the position of slavery in the colonies and into the condition of the poor in the British Isles were being made, there were also investigations into the number of Catholics in Ireland, the degree of illiteracy in England, the effects of punishment upon criminals, and the results of public and private education. It may be thought that the zeal with which the pursuit of information was entered upon was quite at variance with the aloofness postulated formally as the ideal of the state; but the consequences which flowed from these investigations were even more antithetical.

It must not be imagined, as many writers have, that the wide use of Royal Commissions in the middle of the nineteenth century was a resuscitation of a procedure which had completely disappeared during the preceding one hundred and fifty years. This method of inquiry was not rediscovered or recreated by the Whig reformers of the new Parliament of 1833.[1] The dominant party in the Reformed Parliament did not suddenly and rashly restore the practice of an ancient and long-disused institution.

[1] This opinion, which has the apparent approval of the most authoritative authors, and is repeated by all whose researches cease with the standard works of these writers, seems based upon the violent attack on Commissions by J. Toulmin Smith, *Government by Commission Illegal and Pernicious* (1849). This author, whose erroneous legal opinions will be discussed in chapter iv, assumed that the evident malpractices of Commissioners were inherent in the nature and constitution of Commissions and were the distinctive feature of Whig rule.

The revival of Royal Commissions did not, therefore, come as a shock or a surprise to contemporaries in the years following 1832; in fact, the significance of the organ of investigation escaped notice for a number of years.[2]

The reasons for this are twofold. In the first place, Royal Commissions of Inquiry, both statutory and prerogative, had never completely lapsed; they had continued in occasional use as special agencies for the investigation of unusually important subjects upon which information was desired. The subjects which were deemed appropriate for such a method of inquiry were those relating to the administrative departments of government or to other topics which circumstances indicated to be incapable of proper investigation by parliamentary committees. Several Commissions had been appointed in the last decades of the eighteenth century, e.g., those upon Crown forests and upon the American loyalists. Perhaps the most important of these inquiries was that set up to audit the public accounts in 1780 (following earlier ones in 1702 and 1711). Many of the recommendations of this latter Commission reached the statute book; later, after a select committee had sat on the same subject in 1822, the Commission was revived by the Grey Ministry of 1830.

[2] Accepting the accustomed view, the present writers made a careful study of the debates of the Reform Parliament in order to discover the earliest objections to this procedure. There were hardly any to be found. Criticism of individual Commissions was made, but there was no general attack upon this method of inquiry, as there was upon the committee system. Cf. the debates in 1831–32 on the Law Inquiry Commission (July 18) and on the Poor Law Committee (February 1–2) with Peel's protest respecting Commission costs in 1834 (*Parliamentary Debates*, New Series, XXV, 341) and the objection to the increased number of committees (*ibid.*, p. 1128). For criticism of the inquiry into Municipal Corporations, *vide infra*, pp. 107–8.

A very noticeable revival of the procedure by Commission of Inquiry took place after 1800. In the thirty-two years from 1800 to 1831 some sixty or more Commissions of Inquiry were appointed, some with statutory authority, most without,[3] listed in Table I.

Many of these Commissions were engaged upon inquiries of considerable magnitude. Among those which may be mentioned are those upon the administration of justice in England, Scotland, and Ireland, which issued ten, seventeen, and thirteen reports, respectively (1806–1825); the army (19 reports, 1806–1816); the navy (14 reports, 1803–1806); customs and excise (16 reports, 1820–1824); and education and charities in England and Ireland (which, respectively, issued 13 reports after 1819, 14 from 1809 to 1812). These Commissions were bodies which existed over a period of years and were therefore able to take their time in the investigation of the questions put to them and the careful consideration of the evidence they received. One such body, the Commission on the Common Law, continued long into the reform period, and its reports (the first in 1829 on the practice and proceedings of the supreme courts of com-

[3] These Commissions are listed in *Parliamentary Papers* which have not been noticed by other writers on the subject. One reason for this is that the first of these lists is concealed in the appendix to a report of a select committee with the misleading name, "Committee on Committee Rooms and Papers." The duties of the committee were wider than its name implied, for it was concerned not only with the shortage of committee rooms but also with the arrangement of printed papers and the republication of those which had not been reissued earlier in the century. The Third Report (*Parliamentary Papers*, No. 516, 1825) contained in Appendix III a list of Commission reports. There is less excuse for the neglect of the other lists of Royal Commissions, with their reports and expenses. A complete list follows: 1825, *Parliamentary Papers*, No. 516, App. III [years 1786–1824]; 1826–27, *ibid.*, No. 301 [1806–1826]; 1829, *ibid.*, No. 212 [1827–1828]; 1830, *ibid.*, No. 379 [1829]; 1832, *ibid.*, No. 512 [1830–1831].

mon law, the second on real property in 1833, etc.) were of distinct influence in the reformation of the legal system.

TABLE I

ROYAL COMMISSIONS OF INQUIRY PRIOR TO 1832

1. Public Records of Great Britain, 1800–1819*
2. Naval Inquiry (frauds and abuses), 1803–1806
3. Fees, Perquisites, etc., of Public Offices in Ireland, 1806–1814
4. Dublin Paving, 1806
5. Public Expenditure in Military Departments, 1806–1816
6. Princess of Wales, 1806
7. Revision of Civil Affairs of the Navy, 1806–1809
8. Irish Schools, 1807–1812
9. Cold Bath Fields Prison, 1808
10. Windsor Forest, 1809–1815
11. New Forest, 1809–1810
12. Bogs in Ireland, 1809–1814
13. Scottish Courts of Justice, 1810, 1805–1808, 1821–1824
14. Saleable Offices in the Law Courts, 1810
15. Public Records in Ireland, 1811–1830
16. Election of Jurats in Jersey, 1812
17. State of Malta, 1812
18. Office of Works, 1812
19. Lincoln Gaol, 1812
20. Lancaster Gaol, 1812
21. Claims of Creditors of the Late Royal Canal Company in Ireland, 1813–1816
22. Irish Courts of Justice, 1815–1831
23. English Courts of Justice, 1815–1818, 1821–1824
24. Laws of Guernsey, 1816
25. Custom and Excise, 1817–1824
26. English and Welsh Charities for Education, etc., of the Poor, 1818–1835
27. State of the Fleet and Marshalsea Prisons, 1819
28. Princess of Wales, 1819
29. Prevention of Forgery of Banknotes, 1819–1820
30. Uniform Weights and Measures, 1819–1821
31. State of the New South Wales, 1819–1822

* The dates of appointment are often hard to ascertain. These dates represent either first and last reports, or years during which expenses of the Commissions are reported.

32. Ilchester Gaol, 1821–1822
33. Captured Negroes in West Indies and British North America, 1821–1824
34. Irish Public Revenue Collection, 1821–1825
35. Land Revenue in Ireland, 1821
36. Irish Fisheries, 1821–1825
37. New Churches in England, 1821–1824
38. Criminal Law in the Leeward Islands, 1822–1824
39. State of the Settlements at the Cape, Ceylon, and Mauritius, 1823–1831
40. Accidents in Gaslight Establishments, 1823
41. Holyhead Roads, 1824–1825
42. Chancery, 1824
43. Irish Schools, 1824
44. Criminal Administration in the West Indies, 1824–1829
45. New Churches in the Highlands, 1825
46. Laws, etc., of Sierra Leone, 1825
47. Jury Trial in Civil Causes in Scotland, 1827–1828
48. Scottish Universities and Colleges, 1827–1831
49. Water Supply of the Metropolis, 1827–1828
50. Real Property Law, 1828–1832
51. Courts of Common Law, 1828–1832
52. Mode of Keeping Public Accounts, 1829–1831
53. Ecclestiastical Courts, England, 1830
54. Ecclesiastical Courts, Ireland, 1830
55. Colonial Accounts, 1830
56. Public Accounts (Receipts and Expenditures), 1830
57. Public Accounts in France, Belgium and Holland, 1830
58. Lancaster Law Courts, 1830
59. Public Records, 1831
60. Colonial Emigration Facilities, 1831

But there were also inquiries into more specific and restricted topics, such as numerous colonial problems, prison administration, the office of works, the forgery of bank notes, Irish bogs, Dublin paving, and the alleged misconduct of the Princess of Wales ("secret" inquiries in 1806 and 1819). These disclose the extent of the utilization of this process of inquiry before the date which is usually held to be that of their resurrection. Royal Commissions, then, though not in as frequent use as they were soon to become, were not unknown before 1832. They had never fallen into complete disuse, and their revival as a recognized and admirable organ of governmental investigation had occurred in the generation before the Whigs came into power.

WIDE USE OF SELECT COMMITTEE PROCEDURE AND ITS DEFECTS

A second reason which may fairly be adduced as making easier the increased use of Royal Commissions was the growing criticism of the existing committee system. After 1660 the chief machinery which served Parliament in the preparation and examination of measures for legislative action had been "select committees" and the Committee of the Whole House.

The Committee of the Whole was the regular procedure by which the House of Commons debated the details of measures which were intended to become law. In addition to the Committee of the Whole, which has continued to the present in an unchanged form, there were several other committees which were in reality no different from the Committee of the Whole. These were the grand committees on religion, grievances, courts of justice, trade, and privileges. But the utility of these special varieties had practically ceased by the nineteenth century, and they were dispensed with after 1832.[4] Not until fifty years later (1882) did the English House of Commons make any concession to the widespread Continental and Ameri-

[4] T. E. May, *A Treatise on the Law, Privileges, Proceedings and Usage of Parliament* (13th ed., 1924), pp. 97, 457.

can practice of constituting standing committees; and when this was done the English standing committees were distinctive in membership and purpose. Perhaps it should be added here that on very rare occasions a Committee of the Whole was charged with the conduct of inquiries, witnesses being examined at the bar of the House;[5] but such a proceeding was an inappropriate encroachment on the time of the Chamber, as well as an unwieldy and inefficient mode of investigation.

The other type, namely "select committees," had become by the end of the Hanoverian period the most influential and distinctive device upon which the Houses of Parliament relied for the accomplishment of many functions. Select committees, however, were never completely institutionalized; they were essentially *ad hoc* bodies created for a specific piece of work, such as the consideration of private bills or the elaboration of public bills which had been accepted in principle. More particularly, select committees were used for all manner of inquiries: investigation of a branch of the administration; scrutiny of revenues and expenditures; examination of the methods and consequences of the operation of certain laws; and the study of any subject upon which the Houses desired definite information.

Few disadvantages were experienced with this system during the eighteenth century. The complacency and satisfaction with which the legislators viewed the laws and institutions of England stifled

[5] For example, miscarriage of the fleet before Toulon, 1744; naval failures in America, 1782; conduct of the Duke of York, 1809; expedition to the Scheldt, 1810. None have taken place since the last-named.

all efforts at alteration; and in consequence the century was devoid of any great constructive law-making. But in the first part of the nineteenth century, and especially in the years immediately preceding the Reform Bill, the extension of inquiry by select committee was accompanied by an ever growing body of criticism directed against the committee system.

The wide use which was made of committees in the first quarter of the nineteenth century shows quite clearly that there was no objection to the existence of some machinery of investigation. Although it is difficult to determine exactly the comparative extent of investigations in the eighteenth and nineteenth centuries, it is nevertheless clear that a great and impressive development of the Parliament's function as the Grand Inquest of the Nation was taking place. Whereas the reports of the eighteenth century (1715–1801) which were selected for re-publication occupied only fifteen volumes, this number was soon equaled each year in the next century. In the first third of the nineteenth century over five hundred committees presented printed reports to the Houses of Parliament, the average number being sixteen per annum.[6] In 1840, a year chosen at random, there were twelve volumes devoted exclusively to committee reports; in 1850 there were eleven. Whatever, then, may have been the number of select committees in the earlier centuries, it is apparent that their number was much increased early in the nineteenth century.

[6] The total from 1801 to 1834 is 543 reporting committees—not reports, which numbered even more, as many committees presented several reports. The total has been found by adding the lists of committees placed at the commencement of each subject section of the large index, *Indexes to Reports of the House of Commons, 1801–1834* (1837), 8 vols.

Appreciation of the value of these early inquiries was expressed in the following terms by the select committee which was concerned with the organization of their reports for the use of the members of the House of Commons: "The importance of the subjects that engaged the attention of Parliament during this period renders the Reports of the Committees, by whom the investigations were conducted, of the greatest public interest. In these Reports there is scarcely a subject connected with the Laws, Institutions, Commerce and Morals of the Country, but what will be found treated on: the Administration of Justice, the Privileges of Parliament, the National Church, Arts and Manufacturing, Agriculture and Trade, Criminal Law, Police and Education — all have their place; and it may be observed that on all subjects relating to Arts and Commerce more information will be found in the Reports than of former periods, arising from the superior intelligence of those who are called upon to impart knowledge, the willingness with which it is communicated, and the greater accuracy with which the evidence and documents are prepared."[7]

It is quite evident that, from the 1820's on, parliamentarians were awakening to the desirability and indeed to the necessity of the investigative function as a prelude to public legislative determination of policy. The growing frequency of investigations into the publication of documents and into the accessibility of their subject matter, together with the recurring discussions of procedure and methods of pur-

[7] *Third Report of the Select Committee on Committee Rooms and Printed Papers* (*Parliamentary Papers*, No. 516, 1825), p. 9.

suing public business, not only reveals a recognition of the importance of these inquiries but shows that the statesmen were preparing to take steps to remedy any defects which interfered with their usefulness. Criticism of the select-committee procedure became more vocal and more specific as the procedure was increasingly utilized.

The criticisms of committee procedure, which were uttered on numerous occasions, may be grouped in four major categories, as to tenure, membership, jurisdiction, and politics. With respect to the first of these, tenure, it was frequently urged that the sessional nature of a committee's life resulted in too hurried work, a failure to utilize the benefits of previous investigations, and complete uselessness of the procedure as the end of the session approached. (Sessions at that period lasted from three to five months in the first part of the year.) So far as the second, membership, was concerned, the chief objections centered upon the large size and inexpert and haphazard composition of the committees. (The usual size was twenty-one members, but this was reduced in 1836 to fifteen.) The question of jurisdiction, the third defect, arose occasionally in its legal or constitutional form. In 1805, for example, a Commons committee had the problem of examining the treasurer of the Navy, Lord Melville, who was a peer.[8] But far more important than the inability to compel the attendance of peers was the fact that committees

[8] Upon conference with the Lords the rule was stated to be that the upper chamber "permit the members of their Lordships' House, on their own request, to defend themselves in the House of Commons, if they think fit, on any point in which that House has not previously passed any accusatory or criminatory Resolutions against them." *Report of Select*

were confined in their inquiries to the precincts of Westminster Hall or, by special leave on rare occasions, to other parts of London.[9] The most that could usually be done was to summon witnesses to London or to rely upon petitions and answers to questionnaires circulated through official or semiofficial avenues. Finally, the allegation was made that select committees were often resorted to by the Government as a means of postponing action by satisfying the proponents of a policy with a promise of inquiry, the report of which might be several months off. After 1832 it was properly pointed out on several occasions that this procedure had been a regular feature of the pre-Reform ministries, which had received almost annual committee reports on the poor laws, industrial conditions, crime in Ireland, etc., without resulting legislative action. Since the appointment of many committees sprang from private members' motions, the Ministry often accepted such inquiries or left them to a free vote of the House instead of taking definite responsibility for the investigations and thus assuming the obligation to act on the reports.

LAISSEZ FAIRE AND THE REFORM OF LEGISLATIVE PROCEDURE

In considering the great extension of investigative methods by Royal Commissions in the nineteenth

Committee on the Tenth Report of the Commissioners of Naval Enquiry (*Parliamentary Papers,* No. 140, 1805), Appendix A. No such limitation had been experienced by the Commissioners in their investigation of the noble lord's financial deficiencies.

[9] T. E. May (*op. cit.,* p. 475) cites as an exceptional case a resolution empowering a select committee of the lords on the sweating system to employ an investigator to visit parts of the country. When a committee of the Commons was proposed for government contracts in 1858, with power to sit outside London, objections led to the appointment of a Royal Commission instead.

century, one must direct attention to the important changes which were taking place at that period in the social and political aspects of English life. The fifty years which extended from 1775 to 1825 not only saw the evolution of the industrial system but also witnessed an equally great transformation in economic and political thinking. The year 1776 is noteworthy for the issuance of the American Declaration of Independence; but it is also momentous on account of the publication of Adam Smith's *Wealth of Nations* and Jeremy Bentham's *Fragment on Government.* These three documents, divergent as they may appear in purpose, in reality heralded a new social era. The American Declaration of Independence not merely propounded the theory of the natural rights of the ruled but in consequence of the military success of the War of Independence it demonstrated that such a right was enforceable and might become the foundation of government. And the French Revolution, in addition to bringing this doctrine into practical operation in Europe, had made it the rallying point of republicanism for the rest of the century. At the same time Smith's doctrine of laissez faire had contributed to the new industrialism a theory upon which could be defended the removal of the ancient customary and statutory limitations on manufacturing and mercantile enterprise.[10] Bentham, likewise, though attacking the contract aspect of natural rights, provided a new criterion by which to judge social welfare in the utilitarian principle of "the greatest good of the greatest number." Slowly and hesitat-

[10] Cf. A. V. Dicey, *Lectures on the Relation between Law and Public Opinion in England during the Nineteenth Century* (1914).

ingly the signs of this new mentality began to be observed among English parliamentarians. Gradually there was awakened an unprecedented interest in facts, a worship of statistics, and an insatiable appetite for official reports. Not only did the number, size, and circulation of parliamentary papers increase many fold in the first third of the nineteenth century, but by the middle of the century the annual product was far greater than in all the centuries before 1800.[11] Bacon's dream of an inductive philosophy based upon careful preparation of factual evidence was becoming realized in the realm of social affairs.

The result of the investigation frequently had effects quite contrary to those anticipated. The very facts which everyone expected might demonstrate the admirable features of the new economy revealed serious social defects in the system. The laissez-faire principle, which was at first expected to be accompanied by unlimited advantages after the removal of the former restraints upon free enterprise, was soon revealed as producing incredible evils in factory and coal mine. Committee after committee reported on the conditions, each time with a greater accumu-

[11] In 1801 there were seven volumes of sessional papers; by 1810 the number was fifteen; and in 1824 there were twenty-four. All together in this period of twenty-four years there had been issued 373 volumes. See *Second Report from Committee on Committee Rooms* (*Parliamentary Papers,* No. 515, 1825). After 1850 the annual production was 60–70 volumes, and sometimes considerably higher.

The number of "articles" (i.e., individual papers) printed for the House of Commons had likewise gone up. In 1797–98 there were 104 articles; in 1835 the number was 633. The number of copies of each item did not show such a marked rise on the average—the usual number being 600 in 1797–98 and 1,000 after 1820—but the exceptional cases were more numerous: in the former year only 13 articles had the high issue of 800–1,200; in the latter year 153 articles had from 1,250–1,750 copies and 33 from 2,000 to 3,000 copies. *Report from the Select Committee on Publication of Printed Papers* (*ibid.,* No. 286, 1837), Appendix V, p. 79.

lation of evidence against full freedom of competition. Distrusted as these reports might be, they made it increasingly clear that governmental intervention was undoubtedly necessary and inevitable as the years passed. But the resistance and inertia which had to be overcome were immense. In criticizing today the dilatory acceptance of reform one hundred years ago it is necessary to remember that nineteenth-century legislators had no experience upon which to draw when contriving their remedies. Industrial and social legislation was a novelty and necessarily proceeded slowly, even when its promoters were sure what abuses it was wise to attack.[12] Nevertheless, as a social historian has remarked: "When all is said for the wisdom and inevitableness of a gradual reformation, these industrial and social laws of the nineteenth century, upon which we sometimes plume ourselves, afford a striking example of the patchwork methods which not invariably, but yet too frequently, characterise English reform, its hesitation, and its extravagance of the fear of spending. The title and number of the Acts upon the statute books are imposing; but if we look at their details, we find that lacking in courage and foresight, they failed in varying degrees to achieve their objects."[13] Thus it took numerous bills and committee reports over a period of twenty-five years to secure the passage by the unreformed House of Commons of legislation limiting a child of nine to sixty-nine hours of labor a week, and this only for cotton mills!

[12] Cf. B. L. Hutchins and A. Harrison, *A History of Factory Legislation* (1903), p. 120.

[13] J. Dunlop, *English Apprenticeship and Child Labour: A History* (1912), pp. 286–87.

The political effects of the new social system are well known. The demand for the reduction of the influence of the landed interests and for the admission to the polls of the new urban middle or lower middle classes produced the Reform Movement, which culminated in the passage of the Reform Bill of 1832 despite the opposition of the Tories and of the House of Lords. In the Reformed Parliament, therefore, which met in 1833, there was a large element from the new industrial areas. These new members, together with the "Repeal" section of Irish members (who had come into influence after the enfranchisement of Roman Catholics in 1829), were continually urging the Whig ministry of Earl Grey to further "reforms." Although the Whigs were supposed to embody in themselves the principles of laissez-faire industrialism, they were predisposed to certain types of reform legislation (e.g., for the relief of Dissenters, and for alteration of the forms of local government). At the same time there was a considerable element of liberalism and radicalism in the Whig ranks, the spokesmen of which (Hume, Grote, etc.) were persistent in directing attention to social evils, and were also insistent upon further investigation into many colonial, religious, and educational problems. The Government was thus under constant pressure to translate into statutory form many of the pledges which had been made prior to the passage of the Reform Act.

SELECT COMMITTEES AND CABINET GOVERNMENT

Constitutionally, at this time, it is to be observed that the cabinet system was not fully operative in its modern form. Prior to 1832 the debates in Parliament reveal how little direction was exercised by the Ministry. As neither party possessed a program of definite policies, the Cabinet could afford to leave members of Parliament free to propose legislation which could be dealt with on its merits. The Ministers did not regard it as their function to lead the House of Commons on all issues, and did not take defeat on minor matters seriously; for they reserved the right to ask for a formal vote of confidence before considering it their duty to resign. But after 1830 the Reform Cabinet of Lord Grey, and later Ministries in consequence, found it necessary to give firmer and more definite guidance to the deliberations of the Commons and to control the business of both Houses with increasing rigidity. Professor Redlich, in his monumental work on the procedure of the House of Commons,[14] has shown how the changes in procedure were closely dependent upon and related to the intensification of party lines. By the middle of the century the old phrase "the minister, who conducted the business of the Government in the House of Commons" had quite definitely been replaced by the "leader of the House."[15] The leader of the House was increasingly expected to determine in a very positive sense the conduct of the chamber. From this time on the private motions for select committees had really to secure the endorsement of the Ministry; otherwise

[14] J. Redlich, *The Procedure of the House of Commons* (1908), Vol. II, Part V, "The Relation of Procedure to the Political and Social Structure of the House of Commons."

[15] He was not necessarily, and indeed rarely, Prime Minister, for this gentleman was usually a peer. Redlich (*op. cit.*, I, 70) erroneously dates the phrase quite late. Both phrases are used in the *Annual Register* for 1834, pp. 129 and 335.

they would be rejected by the House. The logical development of this attitude was that the Ministry would treat a motion for inquiry by select committee into a branch of the administration as a matter of confidence. Thus, in 1855, upon the passage of a resolution to appoint a committee to inquire into the condition of the army before Sebastopol, and "into the conduct of those departments of government whose duty it has been to administer to the wants of that army," Lord Aberdeen resigned from office. He was followed by Lord Palmerston with a reconstituted Liberal Cabinet. The committee of inquiry was persisted in by the House, whereupon three members of the Cabinet resigned, one of them, Mr. W. E. Gladstone, explaining: "an enquiry such as is proposed is incompatible with real confidence on the part of Parliament in those who hold executive office, and entirely incompatible with the credit and authority which ought, under all circumstances, to belong to the Ministers of the Crown, whatever party or political creed they may profess."[16]

This opinion of Mr. Gladstone has been condemned by no less an authority than Sir William Anson as "an extreme view," which "seems to put the case too high."[17] But, in the light of the changes which were taking place in the relation of the Ministry to the House of Commons, one must agree with those Cabinet Ministers who chose to resign, for they had been in the previous Cabinet which had been responsible for the Crimean campaign. The time was approaching when the dominance of the Cabinet made com-

[16] *Parliamentary Debates*, 3d series, Vol. 136, p. 1838.

[17] *Law and Custom of the Constitution* (5th ed., 1922), I, 399.

mittees of the House of Commons really agencies for perfecting Government policies; under the Cabinet system there could be no further divergence between the will of the Commons and the will of the Ministry.

But although the long-run tendency of the growing party discipline was to decrease parliamentary initiative and to reduce all organs of the House of Commons to the position of instruments of the Ministry, this development was not immediately apparent. Select committees were, in fact, more extensively used in the fifty years after 1832 than they had been previous to the Reform era. No visible signs of their decline were evident until the very last decade of the century.[18] For the greater part of the Victorian Age, then, select committees not only persisted as parliamentary devices, but continued to be used as (numerically speaking) the most important instrumentality for inquiry purposes.

Meanwhile, it must be admitted that the political influence of the committee reports had gradually been overshadowed by the more impressive, more thorough, and more authoritative reports of Royal Commissioners. As the historian of parliamentary-committee procedure has said: "The importance of parliamentary committees in this particular direction has, however been materially lessened during the nineteenth century by the growing popularity of 'royal commissions' as means for conducting enquiries."[19]

[18] The average annual number of "reporting" committees before 1832 was 16; in 1824, the total number of such committees "appointed" was 23. In 1840, 27 committees reported; in 1870, 30. Meanwhile, the number of committees appointed increased more noticeably, in 1850 numbering 39; in 1880, 44. Not until after 1890 did a continuous decline in the number of select committees take place: in 1890, 39; 1896, 25; 1900, 19.

[19] Redlich, *op. cit.*, II, 193.

RELATIVE ADVANTAGES OF ROYAL COMMISSIONS

Select committees have been displaced by Royal Commissions or by other agencies which will be discussed in a later chapter. In the second quarter of the nineteenth century, however, Royal Commissions and select committees underwent their great growth along parallel lines. The spirit of inquiry which pervaded Parliament found vent after 1830 both in the scores of committees appointed during each session and in the establishment of numerous Commissions.[20] And as the Ministry of the day attained greater and greater control of the time and procedure of the House it was natural for it to reject the use of select committees and to utilize in greater degree the Royal Commission. The reasons for this change are easily ascertainable.

In the first place, it will be recalled that Royal Commissions are instruments of the Crown. By the nineteenth century it was firmly established in English government that the powers of the Crown were exercised by the Ministry. There was, therefore, none of the old hostility of the Parliament to royally constituted Commissions, since the latter were appointed in reality by the Cabinet, which was now an agency of the House of Commons. Commissions were, in view of the admitted defects of committees, the natural weapon by which the Crown acted for investigative purposes; and when the Cabinet, though of parliamentary creation, became the actual wielder of Crown authority, the step to the utilization of the ancient organ of royal power was easy.

[20] From 1831 to 1844 the number of Commissions appointed was 91.

There were sound political reasons for this procedure. As the control of the Commons by the Cabinet tightened through the establishment of disciplined political parties, the ministers could not but feel hindered and limited by the inquiries conducted by the parliamentary mechanism of select committees. Such bodies were chosen in the nineteenth century on a nonpartisan basis, although they were composed of partisan members. The Ministry, however, wanted two things. Where no issue of policy was involved, the Government desired expert inquiry of a nonpartisan type which would produce results they could accept. On the other hand, when the Government did possess a policy which must be preceded by inquiry, they desired to have the investigation made by men who, even if not openly partisan (on their side), were at least sympathetic and not irreconcilable. Select committees could not always provide these conditions. Royal Commissions, on the other hand, could be made definitely expert or impartial when needed or they could be "packed" to any degree desired.

A further political reason for the popularity of Royal Commissions with the Government is to be found in the procedure of establishment. Committees, especially when originating from private members' motions, could not but be regarded as somewhat of a reflection upon the Government. Commissions, on the other hand, sprang from executive action. Thus the Government would forestall criticism of its policy or administration by initiating inquiry by Commission and come through the criticisms more or less unscathed.

All considerations, therefore, indicated that Royal Commissions were more desirable than select committees; and such proved to be the case for many years. It cannot be argued that Commissions avoided all the defects which were found in the committee system; but at least Commissions were not limited by parliamentary time, were not restricted in their *situs,* and were not confined in personnel to the members of the Parliament. "A royal commission," declares Professor Redlich, "has many advantages over a parliamentary committee; it can, while a parliamentary committee cannot, prolong its work beyond the limits of a session, if necessary even for years; and it is possible to appoint scientific experts as members so as to secure a completely impartial treatment of the subject; the consequence is that commissions have largely superseded parliamentary committees when elaborate enquiries have to be made."[21]

ROYAL COMMISSIONS AT THEIR PEAK AFTER 1850

The extent of the use of Royal Commissions after 1830 must not be exaggerated in the numerical sense. All together, in the seventy years from 1830 to 1900, there were created some 388 Royal Commissions of Inquiry—356 if one excludes the special Commissions to investigate bribery[22]—an average over the whole period of a little more than five per annum (see Table II). The period of the greatest activity of Royal

[21] Redlich, *The Procedure of the House of Commons,* II, 193.

[22] In this period there were 32 such election Commissions. In the years immediately following the Reform Act such Commissions were occasionally used, but after 1842 they became a statutory procedure (5 & 6 Victoria, c. 102; 15 & 16 Victoria, c. 57). They occur in the following years: 1843, 1; 1851, 1; 1853, 9; 1860, 1; 1866, 4; 1869, 6; 1875, 2; 1880, 8. Cf. T. E. May, *op. cit.,* p. 647.

TABLE II

COMMISSIONS OF INQUIRY, 1832–1900

Year Created	Number of New Commissions	Most Important Subjects
1832	3	Poor laws, Ecclesiastical revenues (England and Ireland)
1833	11	Criminal law digest, Municipal corporations (England, Scotland, and Ireland), Children in factories, Irish poor, Excise department
1834	4	Religious instruction (Ireland), Post office, St. Helena
1835	9	Church, Military punishment, Parliament plans, Religious instruction (Scotland), Lower Canada grievances, Irish fisheries
1836	8	Registration of vital statistics, Aberdeen and Glasgow Universities, Malta
1837	1	Handloom weavers
1838	3	Military and naval promotion, Canadian rebellion
1839	1	
1840	2	Children in mines
1841	6	Fine arts, Revenue, Irish census, Irish law courts
1842	5	
1843	6	Scotch poor law, Irish lands
1844	1	Frame-work knitters
1845	7	Judicial circuits, Inclosures, Ulster college, Potato disease in Ireland
1846	5	Welsh education
1847	7	Bishoprics, Land titles, Marriage law, British Museum
1848	6	Irish public records, Customs, Westminster Palace
1849	7	Episcopal estates, Redistribution of parishes
1850	5	Superior Court procedure, Chancery, Oxford and Cambridge Universities
1851	4	Dublin University, Ancient laws of Ireland
1852	3	
1853	18	Nine election commissions, Mercantile law digest, County courts, Bankruptcy

Year Created	Number of New Commissions	Most Important Subjects
1854	9	Land-title registration, Military promotion, Irish schools
1855	8	Eastern army supplies, Decimal coinage
1856	7	Army commission purchase
1857	8	Irish colleges, Aberdeen University, Ordinance survey
1858	13	Popular education, Naval recruitment, Militia
1859	10	Licensing (Scotland), Recruiting for army, Chancery evidence, Law, equity, etc., Consolidation
1860	5	Prince Edward Island
1861	5	Endowed schools, Indian law, Irish superior courts
1862	6	Volunteers, Patents, Child labour, Mines, Penal servitude
1863	4	Royal Academy, Fisheries
1864	9	Capital punishment, English education, Scottish schools
1865	8	Marriage law, Railway rates, Jamaica outbreak
1866	8	Law digest, Recruiting, Coal supplies
1867	7	Judicature, Neutrality laws, Weights and measures, Trade unions, Women and children in agriculture, Church ritual, Irish church revenues
1868	9	Scottish courts, Military punishment, Naturalization, Military education, International coinage, Irish education
1869	10	Six elections, Scientific education, Historical manuscripts
1870	5	Army purchase, Friendly societies
1871	4	
1872	4	Oxford and Cambridge Universities, Endowed schools (Scotland)
1873	3	
1874	5	Army promotion, Labour laws
1875	7	Copyright, Vivisection, Factory acts
1876	3	Scottish universities, Muncipal corporations
1877	5	Extradition, London Stock Exchange

Year Created	Number of New Commissions	Most Important Subjects
1878	8	Criminal code, Penal servitude, Scottish public schools
1879	6	Agricultural depression, Wellington College, Mining accidents
1880	12	Eight elections, Colonial ports
1881	5	Transvaal, Ecclesiastical courts, Foreign technical education
1882	5	West Indian finances, Reformatories, Education (Scotland)
1883	5	Highland crofters
1884	4	Mauritius, Housing
1885	2	Depression in trade and industry
1886	8	Gold and silver, Civil establishments, Irish land purchase, Elementary education
1887	3	
1888	4	Highland crofter emigration, London University, Naval and military departments
1889	4	Mining royalties, Vaccination
1890	3	Tuberculosis
1891	5	Tithe redemption, Labour
1892	4	
1893	5	London Government, Agricultural depression, Aged poor
1894	4	Secondary education, Irish financial relations
1895	3	
1896	4	West Indian depression, Local taxation
1897	3	Manual training in primary schools, Irish land acts
1898	5	London University
1899	3	
1900	3	Port of London, South African hospitals

Commissions, as shown by the date of appointment, will be seen to occur not in the years of the Reform Parliament but twenty years later.[23] In the decade

[23] Lists of commissions from 1832 to 1900 can be secured from the following *Parliamentary Papers,* which enumerate them virtually in chronological order: 1834 (291), XLI; 1836 (528, 341), XXVII; 1837 (290),

after 1831 only forty-one new Commissions were appointed, and considerably over half of these belong to the three years 1833 (11), 1835 (9), and 1836 (8). A rise in the number took place in the next decade (1841–1850), when 54 Commissions were created; but it was in the 'fifties (and more particularly from 1850 to 1858) that the peak of the Commission procedure was reached. For fifteen years prior to 1853 the new creations never rose above 7 a year; for seven years after 1853 the number never fell below this point, and the total for the decade was 74. This was the high tide for the century; after this there was a gradual decrease. From 1861 to 1870 the average was 6 a year; from 1871 to 1880 it had fallen to less than 5. The last twenty years saw the number of new Commissions stabilized at four annually.

The numerical increase, therefore, of the Royal Commissions corresponded to and accompanied the increase in the number of select committees noted above as occurring in the middle of the nineteenth century. So also at the end of the century the decline in the use of Royal Commissions preceded that of the select committees by only a few years.

XXXIX; 1837–38 (346), XXXVI; 1839 (432), XXX (supplement), (Scottish only); 1840 (237), XXIX; 1842 (449), XXVI; 1846 (187), XXV; 1847–48 (669), XXXIX; 1850 (720), XXXIII; 1854–55 (284, 210), XLIII (Law commissions only); 1856 (415), XXXVIII; 1859, ii (196), XV; 1862 (317), XXX; 1867 (261), XL; 1887 (342), LXVI; 1888 (426), LXXXI; 1896 (338), LXVIII; 1904 (315), LXIX.

The date is the year in which the *Parliamentary Papers* are collected; 1859, ii means the second session of that year. The number in parentheses is the number of the paper. The Roman numerals indicate the volume in which the papers are bound, for they are not collected in order of issuance.

CHAPTER IV

ROYAL COMMISSIONS AND POLITICS

[Inquiries are] well-fitted for overloading every question with ten or fifteen times the quantity of matter necessary for its consideration.—W. E. GLADSTONE

[Inquiries are] pregnant with prudent and sagacious suggestions for the improvement of the administration of affairs.—B. DISRAELI

LEGALITY OF COMMISSIONS OF INQUIRY

The revival of the use of Royal Commissions in the nineteenth century and the extensive adoption of this procedure for numerous political purposes was never seriously challenged, though it was often criticized. Because the utilization of the commission form of inquiry preceded some of the most distinctive legislative measures of the Reform era, this method of procedure gained the disapproval of many of the opponents of the reforms which resulted from its use. Yet as the inquiry process was employed by both Whig and Tory parties the leaders of neither party were able to condemn the method in absolute terms. And though the evidence, which the Royal Commissions found it necessary to report, was frequently in conflict with the extreme views of both radicals and ultra-conservatives, the support of moderates of both sides of the House of Commons assured the procedure sufficient approval to guarantee its continuance. The irreconcilables—on the ground either of self-interest or of doctrine — remained unconvinced. "There are some, however," wrote one of them, a man who could not resist the opportunity to write a book against Royal Commissions, "who are obstinate and blind enough to think that the present as well as permanent well-being of the community is endangered by this system of Commissions—which forms the one grand characteristic of Whig administration, the mark by which it will be known in history."[1]

The objections which were taken to the system of "crown-appointed" Commissions, among which both those of inquiry and those of administration were comprehended, were twofold: that they were illegal, and that they were—to use an American phrase—"spoils of office." The first of these, illegality, was argued on the seventeenth-century basis. With frequently reiterated quotation from Coke's *Institutes,* it was contended that there were certain fundamental laws of English government which were violated when royally appointed Commissioners were authorized to inquire into or to administer the law in any fashion other than by the common-law proceedings of the courts of justice. The illegality sprang both from the appointment (without parliamentary sanction) of officials who were a charge upon the nation and from their jurisdiction being exercised without the historic protection of jury trial and the "law of the land." The words of Blackstone in the middle of the eighteenth century have already been quoted[2] against the employment of Commissioners and government agents. Toward the close of that century

[1] J. T. Smith, *Government by Commissions Illegal and Pernicious. The Nature and Effects of All Commissions of Inquiry and Other Crown-appointed Commissions. The Constitutional Principles of Taxation; and the Rights, Duties and Importance of Local Self-Government* (1849), p. 20.

[2] *Vide supra,* p. 53.

objection was formally registered in the House of Lords against the statute authorizing the appointment of a board of commissioners for the Crown woods and forests: "3rdly Because the powers of survey given to the commissioners are dangerous to the quiet of the subject, and derogatory to the honour of the Crown."[3]

There is no doubt now that the view that Royal Commissions were illegal was a mistaken one.[4] But it was not until 1850, after the question of legality had been raised in the case of inquiries into municipal corporations (1835)[5] and into Oxford University (1850) that the issue was finally disposed of. At the same time the nature and limits of authority to be

[3] *Protests of the Lords* (Rogers, ed., 1875) II, 217. As created by the act (26 George III, c. 87) the Commissioners were to examine the woods, forests, and land commons of the Crown. They became a permanent administrative board. Lord Loughborough and the other protesting peers feared that by abuse "the tenants of the Crown may be restrained from their accustomed privileges" (p. 218).

[4] *Vide,* however, the rulings of Australian and New Zealand courts, cited by W. H. Moore, "Executive Commissions of Inquiry," *Columbia Law Review,* XIII (1913), 510–11, 520–23.

[5] Protests were entered by peers at several stages of the corporation reform bill. The only one of importance for our purposes is that on August 3, 1835, when Lord Winchilsea and the Duke of Newcastle opposed the motion to hear evidence in support of the bill: "1st Because the Commission under which the Commissioners for inquiring into Municipal Corporations have acted is perfectly illegal and unconstitutional, the Constitution of this country recognising no such arbitrary power as that which has been claimed by the Crown of issuing a Commission without the consent of the Houses of Parliament deeply affecting the hereditary rights, privileges, and properties belonging to the municipal borough towns . . . . 2ndly, Because that, by acknowledging such a principle by hearing evidence this House will establish a precedent of a most dangerous character, which will endanger the security, not only of all existing hereditary rights and privileges, but of every species of property, whether of a public or private character, existing in this country. 3rdly, Because that, however specious the title of this Bill may appear, it is evident to every mind unprejudiced by party feeling, that the object which it is intended to accomplish is the furtherance of that democratic spirit which is at present afloat in this country, and which is aiming at the total subversion of all the civil and religious institutions of the British Empire" (*Protests of the Lords,* III, 153–54).

exercised by Royal Commissions were definitely laid down. The difficulties have arisen from the confusing of the three main types of commissions. Special judicial commissions—"to hear and determine"—confer upon specifically named judges of the regular courts a particular jurisdiction over locality and types of offenses which must be tried in conformity with law. Thus, in 1832, special commissions had been issued to deal with the Reform riots and turbulence in Nottingham and Bristol, and shortly afterward similar proceedings were used in the Irish tithe disorders. Administrative commissions (and boards) have not been created since the Revolution of 1688 except by statute—unless their functions come definitely within the scope of the royal prerogative, as was the case of the commissioners appointed in 1833 to adjudicate upon the losses to British subjects arising from French sequestration of 1793, etc.[6] It is unquestionably true, of course, that many Commissions of Inquiry have shortly given rise to more or less permanent administrative commissions, as in the cases of the Ecclesiastical Commission, the Audit Commission, the Slavery Compensation Commission, the Sanitary Commission, etc.; but in every such example this transformation from inquiry to administration was instituted and authorized by statutory provision.

It was the failure to perceive the essential difference in status between the administrative, judicial, and inquiry types of commission which caused the misreading of ancient history. Accordingly, in 1850,

[6] Strangely enough this commission, which is obviously semi-judicial and semi-administrative in nature, is listed among the Commissions of Inquiry in a return to the House of Commons in 1848. *Parliamentary Papers,* XXXIX, No. 669, 1848.

when the inquiry into Oxford University was resisted by the University, the law officers of the Crown quite properly reported: "The authorities on the subject of Special Royal Commissions relied on . . . . are quite beside the present question."[7] The law officers could see nothing in common between the illegal commissions which had formerly attempted unauthorized taxation, punishment, and criminal inquiry and the Royal Commissions of Inquiry which merely investigated public questions.

[7] The Heads of the Colleges had secured the legal opinion of G. J. Turner, R. Bethell, H. Keating, and J. R. Kenyon to the effect that there was no visitatorial power in the Crown, and that a similar visitation under James II had been declared illegal in the Bill of Rights. Relying upon the early statutes and upon Coke, the opinion concluded: "Considering then that the object of this Commission is Inquiry alone, and that it is not authorised by Parliament, that there is no precedent for such a commission as regards the University, and no judgment of any court of justice establishing any like Commission; considering also the authorities of common law and of Parliament against such Commissions, and that serious mischiefs may ensue from it; we are of the opinion that this Commission is not constitutional or legal, and that it is not such as the University or its Members are bound to obey" (*Report of His Majesty's Commissioners to Inquire into the State, Discipline, Studies, and Revenues of the University and Colleges of Oxford* [1852, Vol. XXII, No. 1482], Appendix, p. 25). The Commission then secured the opinion of Sir John Dodson (Advocate General), Sir A. J. E. Cockburn (Attorney General), and Sir W. P. Wood (Solicitor General) as quoted in the text (*ibid.*, Appendix, p. 32). More particularly it was said: "The commissions prior to that issued by James II, are referred to in the margin of the passages cited in the above opinion from Lord Coke's Reports, and from his fourth Institute. They resolve themselves into, 1stly, Commissions to impose burdens upon particular districts, such as providing vessels, &c. without the authority of Parliament; in other words, illegally taxing the subject by the sole authority of the Crown. 2ndly Commissions armed with power of fine and imprisonment. 3rdly Commissions to hear and determine offences in a manner contrary to law; both established law and tribunals of the land, and establishing new jurisdictions unknown to the law. 4thly Commissions to hear and inquire into offences without determining them;—also a course of proceeding unknown to and contrary to the law."

"It is to this latter sort of commission," the law officers continue, "that Coke refers in his Twelfth Report, page 31 (as is plain when the whole passage is cited) when he says, 'No such Commission was ever seen to enquire, i.e. of crimes'. And it is to such a Commission that he applies the remark that 'A man may be unjustly accused by false evidence, and shall not have any remedy'."

Yet there was one subject upon which clarification was secured respecting the powers of Commissions of Inquiry. The royal warrant of appointment usually contained—and does still usually contain—a grant of full power to summon such persons as shall be judged likely to afford any information upon the topic, and to call for, have access to, and to examine all such books, documents, and records as may afford the fullest information.[8] Was a Commission of Inquiry entitled to compel the attendance of witnesses by simple virtue of the prerogative of the Crown? Most warrants of appointment are worded as though this were so. But it has no legal foundation; no person can be subjected to compulsion in order to induce testimony except by statute. This question was first broached when the Royal Commission upon Municipal Corporations was appointed in 1835. Chief among the public bodies which resisted the inquiry was the Merchant Tailors' Company,[9] which took legal advice and refused to "give any information whatever to the commissioners."[10] While professing apprehensions about "a roving commission to inquire for griev-

[8] These phrases are taken from the Commission issued in 1919 for the investigation of Oxford and Cambridge Universities. (Perhaps it should be added that there had been an earlier Commission in 1872.) The 1919 Commission held out a bait—it was to consider applications made by these two non-state institutions for financial assistance from the state. Even so, certain colleges refused to open their books to the Commission. The *Report* was presented in 1922 (*Parliamentary Papers,* Vol. X, Cmd. 1588). Nearly all warrants of appointment confirm these words.

[9] The reason for this action lay in the Government's unsuccessful attempt, made earlier in the year, to upset the existing government of the Company. *Quo warranto* proceedings failed to oust the Master of the Company on the ground of illegality in the four-hundred-year-old system of election. *King* v. *Attwood,* reported in *Annual Register,* 1933, Part ii, p. 19.

[10] *Ibid.,* pp. 157–59, which contains the opinion of Sir James Scarlett (later Lord Abinger), concurred in by Mr. Follett and Mr. Rennell.

ances," they did not go as far as Coke had done in condemning outright the royal power to appoint "commissioners to inquiry only, and not to determine." Instead, the legal opinion was advanced that, "by common law, which is the right of the subject, no man can be compelled to disclose any matter that may expose himself to peril, except in a due course of justice. . . . . Commissioners for inquiry may be the source of much useful information furnished voluntarily . . . . but . . . . it is not consistent with the law or the liberty of the subject, that commissioners . . . . should be endued with a power of compulsion either for the disclosure of facts or the attendance of witnesses. The address of the House of Commons, as the law now stands, can add nothing to their validity." This view was accepted by the law officers of the Crown seventeen years later in the Oxford University dispute, in the course of which the Commission of Inquiry was defined as "a Commission issued by the Crown for the purpose of obtaining information on a matter of public concern, without the assumption of any compulsory powers, and whose sole authority is derived from the respect with which it may be expected that a Royal Commission will be treated by Her Majesty's subjects, more especially by public bodies and constituted authorities."[11]

Royal Commissions, then, despite the terms in which the warrant might be couched, have no inherent power of compulsion. In this respect they were in a less favorable position than the committees of

[11] *Report* on Oxford University, cited in footnote 8. Smith was therefore correct in so far as compulsory jurisdiction was concerned; he had noted that no Commission had ever attempted to force the presentation of documents (*op. cit.*, p. 211).

the Houses of Parliament, whose powers of enforcing attendance of witnesses and production of documents were covered by parliamentary privilege.[12] Full powers in these respects could, of course, be conferred by statute for the individual Commission; and such was occasionally done. It was not until 1921 that the Tribunals of Inquiry (Evidence) Act[13] granted any executive committee or Commission of Inquiry these powers (designated as the rights and privileges that are vested in the High Court) upon the passage by both Houses of Parliament of a resolution declaring the subject matter of the inquiry to be of urgent public importance.

No objection can now be made to the use of Royal Commissions upon constitutional grounds. The cleavage between the Crown and Parliament has been completely reconciled by ministerial exercise of royal powers; and the "separation of powers," though it may still be legal theory, has been superseded by the harmonizing principles of the cabinet system. A "crown-appointed" or "royal" commission is only in a formal sense a monarchical weapon; in practice it is quite clearly and undeniably an agency of ministers who possess a majority in the House of Commons. A Royal Commission is thus every whit as much a parliamentary device as is a select committee of either House. The main feature of English government being the conduct of the Government by

[12] But committees did not possess the right to examine witnesses upon oath. This was first extended to the committees for trying disputed election returns by the Grenville Act, 1770. When Commissions took over this function, they were given a similar power. All committees now have the authority to administer oaths. 34 & 35 Victoria, c. 83 (1871).

[13] II George V, c. 7.

ministers who possess the confidence of the House of Commons, the allegation that this ancient royal procedure is unconstitutional in any sense becomes ludicrous. "The constitutional right of the Crown to issue commissions of inquiry has indeed been questioned," remarked Alpheus Todd fifty years ago,[14] "but mainly for reasons which, however weighty they might have been so long as prerogative government existed, are wholly inapplicable to our present political system. Since the establishment of ministerial responsibility, commissions have become a recognised part of our governmental machinery, and it is freely admitted that, when confined to matters of legitimate inquiry, they serve a most useful and beneficial purpose."

EARLY ACCUSATION OF JOBBERY AND CORRUPTION

Criticism of Royal Commissions came not only from those whose interests were affected by the inquiries set on foot by the Government but also from those who felt disturbed at the "centralizing" tendency of such inquiries. These critics felt the investigations were essentially a part of centralization, and feared them as preparatory to new restrictions upon individual rights and local self-government. In their eyes, Commissions—of both the administrative and the investigative type—were little more than opportunities for patronage and jobbery. The new expansion of government enterprise was according to this view not a step in the direction of progress but an additional method of distributing offices and sinecures. The old institutions and the old ways of conducting

[14] *Parliamentary Government in England* (Walpole, ed., 1892), II, 94.

government, it was declared, were distasteful to the reformers because "they give no place to Commissioners and Inspectors; therefore they must be obsolete, and not adapted to the spirit of the age."[15] After the Municipal Corporation Act one critic did not hesitate to aver that "a Commission of Inquiry is an infinitely more corrupt institution, more jobbing and more mischievous, than any close corporation that ever existed";[16] and the Public Health Bill was described as "a bill to legalise universal jobbing, to create universal patronage. Hence an army of government appointed inspectors to enforce upon the land all the narrow and procrustean schemes and crotchets of a central board."[17]

It might be thought that no credence should be given to such sweeping assertions. Unfortunately, however, the diatribes of the critics were based upon a foundation of fact sufficient to provide at least partial justification for their claims. There were too many examples illustrative of the accusations for them to be neglected. The criticisms were largely threefold: that the Commission system provided an enormous opportunity for patronage; that the accounts were "padded"; and that the Government was the prey of interested as well as disinterested theorists.

It must be remembered that the use of Commissions for informational purposes, as well as for administrative control, was very largely in direct opposition to the theories and the economic and social

[15] J. T. Smith, *op. cit.*, p. 17.
[16] *Ibid.*, p. 201.
[17] *Ibid.*, p. 298.

interests of the dominant groups at the middle of the nineteenth century. "Between 1830 and 1840," says Professor Dicey,[18] "the issue between individualists and collectivists was fairly joined." Yet, though declaring that the "enlightened opinion of 1832" governed the action of Parliament for some thirty or forty years, he has to admit not only that the "Benthamite reformers have never had a perfectly fair chance of bringing their policy to a successful issue"[19] but that many of the reforms were accomplished not by Whig reformers, but by "Tory philanthropists."[20] The fact is, of course, that the party lines were only general indications of the individualist-collectivist cleavage. There were laissez-faire supporters among both Whigs and Tories; and there were "social reform" radicals on the Whig side as there were "philanthropists" among the Tories. Under the circumstances one must wonder that state intervention progressed at all, for there is no doubt that the hesitations and hindrances experienced in attaining government regulation by administrative machinery—when the need for it was established by inquiry—is clearly to be traced to the interested parties who would be inconvenienced and to the general frame of mind of that period.

The critics of innovation attributed all forms of interference to the malevolence or malfeasance of the Government of the day, and particularly to the Whig Ministries which did not adhere to the strict

[18] *Lectures on the Relation between Law and Public Opinion in England during the Nineteenth Century* (2d ed., 1914), p. 217.

[19] *Ibid.*, p. 218 n.

[20] *Ibid.*, pp. 220–40.

rule of Benthamite philosophy. Thus it was said of them: "They make, indeed, their readiness to try any new experiment their boast. They thus become the easy dupes of every vain promulgator of idle crotchets or interested disseminator of specious quackery; and one may depend with pretty confident certainty upon setting on foot one of those numerous experiments of which the beginning is always a 'Commission of Inquiry,' and the end a 'General Board' of paid Commissioners."[21]

That the growth of regulation of industrial life by the state should be the occasion for considerable patronage and jobbery may be admitted. Two things should be noted in explanation of the expansion of offices and of the criticism which flowed from it. On the one hand, there was arising in the first half of the nineteenth century, as a result of the influence of Benthamism and of business opinion, a reaction against the old patronage system.[22] And, on the other hand, there was at that time no efficient and expert civil service capable of or equipped for securing the

[21] Smith, *op. cit.*, p. 17. The literature of the period is filled with similar opinions; the frequent quotations are made from Smith only because he connected the "reforming" tendency with Royal Commissions.

Such views must strike a responsive chord in the United States today, for identical criticisms have been directed against the "New Deal" policy of the Roosevelt administration. Party lines have been obscured by the Democratic policy. There are New Deal Republicans as well as New Deal Democrats; and there are anti-New Deal Democrats who joined the Republicans in opposing the re-election of President F. D. Roosevelt. Government intervention has been denounced as a violation of the Constitutional rights of the states and of the individual; the numerous (alphabetically designated) boards and commissions have been pictured as devices for patronage and spoils and not of mere administrative convenience; and the New Deal principles, which were professedly designed to introduce a regulated national economy, have been ridiculed as the "crack-pot" schemes of impractical "brain-trusters."

[22] The subject of sinecures, for instance, had exercised the minds of parliamentarians in 1810–1812, and particularly after 1830. *Vide Parliamentary Papers*, 1830–31, Vol. III, No. 322, and 1833, Vol. XII, No. 671.

information desired or for administering the new policies as they were determined upon. In the very nature of the case, then, the cry of jobbery would be raised no matter what the system of appointment.

As might be expected the critics of the Government made rather fantastic statements. The full force of the exaggeration was derived from confusing investigating Commissions with administrative boards. Thus it was declared that in the twelve years between 1832 and 1844 there had been 150 Commissions in operation,[23] a number which has been cited by most writers since that time. That there were a large number is technically true (over 160, in fact); but this number gives a wrong impression, since it includes the numerous renewals of Commissions (in 1835 there were seven renewals and seven new creations), and ten Commissions which had continued from before the Reform Parliament, as well as the permanent or semi-permanent Commissions which were turning into administrative bodies. The actual number of Commissions of Inquiry for this period is, not 150, but 61; and for the twenty years from 1831 to 1850 the total is only 101—an average of five a year.

There is no doubt that the establishment of the numerous administrative commissions did provide a very considerable number of well-paid posts. There was justification for the ridicule of the "Whig triumviri, the solution of all difficulties, political, social, and moral"; "the Trinity of the Whigs, viz. three commissioners, each receiving, as may be, one, two, or three thousand a year"; and the "three paid com-

[23] *Vide* Smith, *op. cit.*, pp. 23–28.

missioners, being three Whig gentlemen of agreeable politics and easy disposition, and also very thick with the Whig aristocracy." It provided opportunity for so noted a journalist as the Rev. Sydney Smith, himself a Whig reformer, to indulge his pen in attacking the ecclesiastical commission: "Their [the Whig Government's] favourite human animal, the barrister of six years' standing, would be called into action. The whole earth is, in fact, in commission, and the human race, saved from the flood, are delivered over to the barristers of six years' standing. The *onus probandi* now lies upon any man who says he is not a commissioner; the only doubt of seeing a new man among the Whigs is, not whether he is a commissioner or not, but whether it is tithe, poor-laws, boundaries of boroughs, church leases, charities, or any of the thousand concerns, which are now worked by commissioners, to the comfort and satisfaction of mankind, who seem in these days to have found out the real secret of life—the one thing wanting to sublunary happiness—the great principle of commission, and six years' barristration."[24]

[24] "Second Letter to Archdeacon Singleton" (*Works of Sydney Smith*, numerous editions). Smith's chief objection to the Ecclesiastical Commission seems to have been that no members of the lesser clergy were on the board. It may be remarked here that he did not hesitate to write a letter to Lord Brougham, after the latter became Lord Chancellor, in which he expressed in no uncertain terms his expectation of promotion. A recent biographer refers to this appeal for patronage as a "manly" letter. Cf. letters quoted in H. Pearson, *The Smith of Smiths* (1935), pp. 206–7, and G. W. E. Russell, *Sydney Smith* (1904), pp. 124–25.

While on the personal note it should be pointed out that J. T. Smith was similarly disgruntled by the treatment he had received by officialdom and commissioners; and in particular by the disregard of his opinions by the metropolitan sanitary commission. The account he gives of his interrogation by the Commission leaves one in serious doubt whether he was really a victim or merely a bigot. Smith, *op. cit.*, pp. 221–28, 359–65.

The most noteworthy expansion took place under the Charities Commission, which required 32 commissioners, of whom 22 were "sti-

But with few exceptions, each of which was relentlessly displayed and pilloried, the members of Commissions of Inquiry served without remuneration or with mere expense allowances. In the cases of professional men, and particularly of the lawyers, compensation was usually made: e.g., the Criminal Law Commissioners received £800 a year for services which were admittedly "spare time," and after having been in existence for fifteen years were subjected to criticism by a select committee of the House of Commons.[25] But, as already remarked, examples of this kind were the exception and not the rule. Moreover, complaints respecting the cost of Commissions were not new in 1832. The Commission of Law Inquiry, consisting of twelve members at £1,200 a year, had cost £50,000 by 1830.[26] And it was asserted at that time that "one notable Scotch canal commission had swallowed up more money than all the other commissions put together from the year 1807 down to a very recent period, and had it not been for the fortu-

pendiary" (among them being Edward Romilly and James Hume) at £1,000 each for the entire work of the Commission, with allowance of £20 a day for expenses. The Poor Law Commission included three commissioners for England at £2,000 a year, a secretary at £1,200, and 21 assistant commissioners at £700; for Ireland, one-third of this number at the same rates; and for Scotland, one commissioner at £2,000, and an assistant at £1,200, and a secretary at £1,000. Next in importance was the Tithe Commission, with three commissioners at £1,500, and eleven assistants and a secretary at £800 apiece. The Copyhold and Enclosure commissioners were members of other Commissions and generally received no additional compensation. Other Commissions of the day were the Audit, Public Works Loans, Lunacy, Emigration Board, Railways, and Slave Trade. There was therefore considerable ground for the accusation of patronage.

[25] The committee thought the sum of £800 a year "for work performed at their leisure hours a large remuneration, and request the attention of the government to urge a speedy termination of their labours" (*Report of the Select Committee on Miscellaneous Expenditures,* [Vol. XVIII, No. 543, 1848], p. xxxvi).

[26] Hansard's *Parliamentary Debates,* New Series, Vol. 25, pp. 290–91.

nate discovery of steam navigation, the chances were that the whole of the money would have gone to the bottom of the Canal."[27] Generally speaking, however, the practice was, and has continued to the present time, to regard Commissions of Inquiry as voluntary public services, without compensation, and with limited expense allowances.[28]

The charge that the accounts of the Royal Commissions were improperly if not fraudulently reported is likewise an exaggeration. It is true that parliamentary control over expenditures in all the government services was at that time below the level which is now maintained. The careful system of audit, to which the prevention of fraud and jobbery may largely be attributed, had not come into full and efficient operation. But the most extreme allegation that can be made against Commissions of Inquiry is that the reported expenses omitted the costs of printing and of witnesses' compensation — these being charged up elsewhere. To deduce from this that the purpose was simply "to get up a case for increasing government patronage"[29] is ludicrous. Yet some color of justification was provided by the fact that the printing expenses often exceeded the other costs of the Commissions. The criticism directed against the cost of witnesses and printing was no more true for the Commissions than for other parliamentary committees. The same compensation was paid for Com-

[27] *Ibid.*, p. 291.

[28] Anxiety respecting enlargement of expenses was shown by the call for publication of lists of Commissions with salaries and other expenses. The early lists (*supra*, p. 78) regularly contain denials by nearly all Commissions that their members were paid, e.g., in particular, *Parliamentary Papers*, No. 528, 1836.

[29] J. T. Smith, *op. cit.*, p. 218.

mission witnesses as for committee witnesses;[30] and the greater expense of printing was but a part of the increased cost of all government printing.[31] Nevertheless, whether as a result of this adverse criticism of costs or as a result of greater experience and efficiency, the reported expenses of Commissions (again omitting printing costs, etc.) were for the ensuing twenty years (1851–1870) only half of what they had been in the first twenty years (1831–1850), although the second period is that in which the greatest number of new Commissions were established.[32] The conclusion seems justified that while actual corruption cannot be alleged, the first years of "reform" Royal Commissions were perhaps twice as expensive as they need have been, and that the £60,000 to £70,000 a year which they cost (£40,000 of it being expenses without witnesses and printing) could easily have been halved.

[30] At that time there was no recognized table of fees payable to witnesses appearing before committees of the House of Commons. Witnesses were generally paid in accordance with the House of Lords' table: physicians, barristers, and engineers, three guineas a day; solicitors and surveyors, two guineas; clergymen and "other gentlemen," one guinea; tradesmen, one pound; mechanics, fifteen shillings; laborers, and "persons of the lower class," from five to seven shillings a day. *Report .... on Miscellaneous Expenditures,* Vol. XVIII (1848), Part I, p. 49.

[31] Smith quotes this report, query 823, to show that Commissions of Inquiry were the major cause of the increased cost. But another equally authoritative witness answered query 899 by remarking that the greatest increase arose from the parliamentary inquiries relating to private-bill proceedings. This is an example of the fallacy which results from "selective" quotation. C. E. Trevelyan replied to query 1095: "The great increase under the head of printing has been Parliamentary printing and over that the Treasury has no control."

It should be remarked here that the present practice is for each report to contain a statement of the cost of its printing.

[32] From 1831 to 1848 the reported expenditures were £648,272; from the last date to 1867 an additional £323,427 had been spent, making a total to that time of £971,699. These figures are taken from the respective returns of Royal Commissions presented to Parliament in 1848 and 1867.

COMMISSIONS IN THE REFORM AGE

It may now be accepted that Royal Commissions are a legitimate method of inquiry and that, though this method is of great antiquity, it has proved a modern convenience from which all taint of jobbery has been completely removed. There remain for discussion the occasions upon which they are used, the purposes which lead to their establishment, and the benefits which ensue from employing them.

All Commissions of Inquiry are professedly appointed for the purpose of investigating a subject upon which sufficient precise knowledge is lacking. "We are unanimous," reported the Departmental Committee on the Procedure of Royal Commissions,[33] "in believing that the appointment of Royal Commissions is useful for the elucidation of difficult subjects which are attracting public attention, but in regard to which the information is not sufficiently accurate to form a preliminary to legislation." The reality of this intention has been questioned in a considerable proportion of the inquiries set on foot. However, it may be asserted with confidence that the need of inquisitional search for facts is recognized not only by Government personnel but also by the general public in the greater number of cases of Commissions of Inquiry. This may be so even when the Government policy is openly acknowledged to involve proposals for legislation upon the particular subject to be investigated. For even when a reform or change has become imperative and has, indeed, been decided

[33] *Report of the Departmental Committee on the Procedure of Royal Commissions* (1910, Cd. 5235), p. 6; hereafter cited as *Balfour Report.*

upon by the Cabinet, it is evident that constructive and sound legislation can result only from careful examination of the existing situation and the consequences which may be expected to follow the solution which is contemplated. Nor, for that matter, does the existence of a considerable controversial literature upon a current topic make superfluous a new and comparatively impartial survey of all evidence and opinion respecting the problem to be dealt with. It is only the extreme dogmatist and the interested fanatic who can aver with satisfaction that further serious inquiry of the complicated social problems of the day will be useless or dangerous.

Striking examples of the relation between investigation by Royal Commissions and the political opinions of the Ministry of the day may be found at any period; but the years immediately preceding and succeeding the Great Reform are especially worthy of attention. Two causes lend a particular significance to the early 1830's. In the first place, it was a period of distinctive legal and political change. In the second place, the Reform Ministries of Grey and Melbourne utilized Commissions of Inquiry to a greater extent than had hitherto been customary. The Reform Parliament of 1833 was not merely the first Parliament elected under the reformed system of representation; it was also the first "reforming" Parliament. The Reform Parliament was elected in the full enthusiasm of dawning liberalism (Adam Smith's laissez-faire, the revolutionary "natural rights," and Bentham's utilitarianism). Members of Parliament were therefore pledged to a great many reforms, such as reduced taxation, relief of Dissenters from discrimination, factory regulations, etc. The Reform Ministries were accordingly subjected to considerable pressure from various groups of their supporters. "The Government that in five years recast our municipal as well as our parliamentary institutions, passed the new Poor Law and the first effective Factory Act, and abolished negro slavery, made more lasting change in the British world than any other Cabinet has done since Stuart times."[34] And in so doing, although they did not create or "discover" the device of Royal Commissions, it must be admitted that the Reform Cabinets did at least restore them to a prominence which had not been theirs for a century and a half. One of the chief reasons for doing this was the lack of homogeneity in the ranks of the Government's supporters. When Grey had formed his Ministry in 1830 he had attempted to fuse the Canningites and the reforming Tories with the old Whigs and more recent Radicals. In consequence, not having a systematic body of accepted principles expressed in a party program or built up by tradition, the Ministers not only had to compromise among themselves but had also to conciliate their partisans as far as possible. The procedure most effectively utilized for this purpose was the holding of inquiries by Royal Commissions. "Because law-making of a character so new and comprehensive required a closer examination of complex facts than busy Ministers could give, Lord Grey's Government made the appointment of Royal Commissions the customary prelude to legislation. The lines followed by the Municipal Reform Act, the Factory Act

[34] G. M. Trevelyan, *British History in the Nineteenth Century, 1782–1901* (1922), p. 242.

and the new Poor Law were all traced out beforehand by Commissioners, who had been selected not on account of their official experience or political weight, but as vigorous and able men, usually of known Benthamite proclivities."[35]

Lord Grey and the Whigs first came into office in November 1830. The next two years were chiefly devoted to the struggle for the passage of the reform of parliamentary representation. Reform of Parliament, the one thing upon which all the Government's supporters were united, was never subjected to inquiry by Commissioners but was always treated as a strictly party question. Accordingly, all three bills went through the procedure of the Committee of the Whole. It was defeat in Committee of the Whole that led the Ministry to dissolve Parliament in April 1831. When the reformers were returned with a great majority, the second bill was introduced and passed, only to be rejected by the House of Lords in October of that year. At the next session (March 1832) the third Reform Bill (together with the Irish and Scottish bills for the same purpose) was passed by the House of Commons. After a second defeat in the House of Lords, the Ministry resigned. It resumed office—Wellington and Peel having failed to form a Cabinet—only when given the royal promise of sufficient new peerage creations to carry the bill. Under this threat the bill was carried in the House of Lords on June 4. The last of the unreformed Parliaments came to an end in the final month of the year; hence it was not until 1833 that the Reform Cabinet had a Reform Parliament to carry out its program.

[35] Trevelyan, *op. cit.*, pp. 242–43.

Up to this time (1833) the Government had been too busily occupied with the fight for the Great Reform to be much concerned with other matters. In 1831 only two Commissions of Inquiry had been set up—one-third the number constituted by the Wellington Ministry of the year before. Of these two Commissions, one was a revival of the earlier Public Records Commission, and the other (Colonial Emigration Facilities) gradually turned into a semi-permanent administrative agency. The following year (1832) three Commissions were appointed, but, of these, two had the same subject (Ecclesiastical Revenues) each being concerned with one of the two major divisions of the United Kingdom. From the reports of the Commission on Ecclesiastical Revenues and Patronage in England and Wales there flowed the attempt to reorganize the tithe payment system, to renovate the property rights of the Church, and, finally, to provide a permanent body concerned with the physical interests of the Establishment, the Ecclesiastical Commissioners (1836).[36] The English Commission, however, was chiefly significant as indicating the need, felt by the most ardent supporters of the Church, of making changes to meet the altered social circumstances of the day. Even greater in importance was the Irish Commission, of which more will be said later.

The third Commission of 1832 was to study the practical operation of the laws for the relief of the poor in England and Wales. The subject of poor relief was not new, for it had been agitated in increasing degree for the previous fifty years. Regarded

[36] 6 & 7 William IV, amended by 3 and 4 Victoria, c. 113.

from any angle the law was bad, especially in view of the Speenhamland system of supplementing wages according to the price of bread and the size of the laborer's family. Furthermore, the administration was bad, for it "made the greenroom of Quarter Sessions and its members, the Justices, a new centre of arbitrary and irresponsible power, and a non-representative taxative majority."[37] Both of these aspects were anathema to the Benthamite reformer. Numerous select committees had investigated the matter previously, but the vested interests and the inertia of conservatism had resisted any action. In 1832, in answer to the question whether the ministry was prepared "to bring forward on their own responsibility, any measure for the purpose of amelioration in the Poor Laws of this country," it was stated that, after examining the evidence and reports of committees, the Government was not yet certain as to the proper procedure. The gentlemen on previous committees were declared to have had preconceived notions on the subject, and to have lacked knowledge of the several systems which prevailed in different parts of the country. This knowledge the Ministry felt was essential before any measures could be recommended. They proposed therefore to establish an investigation to be conducted "on the spot" in order to find out the effects of the different systems as they existed; after which, the Ministry would decide what action, if any, was to be taken.[38]

The researches of the Commission, which reported

[37] C. G. Robertson, *England under the Hanoverians* (1912), p. 355.

[38] *Parliamentary Debates*, 3d series, Vol. IX (February 1), pp. 1097–99.

in 1834,[39] revealed clearly the alarming conditions resulting from employers using poor relief as an excuse for less-than-subsistence wages and from workers' knowledge that some aid was always forthcoming in proportion to the size of the families. The Government accepted in large degree the recommendations which were deeply influenced by an ardent Benthamite among the assistant-commissioners,[40] and the resultant act[41] was a revolutionary departure from the policy which had evolved since the time of Elizabeth. Although there have been, since that time, nearly a hundred reports from the numerous bodies concerned with administration and investigation of poor laws, the principles of "indoor" relief administered under central control through poor-law districts and "unions" remained basically the same until the twentieth century saw their implementation by further forms of unemployment insurance and old-age pensions. A permanent Poor Law Commission (followed in 1847 by a Poor Law Board, which in turn was displaced by the Local Government Board in 1917) continued the enforcement throughout the rest of the century. "No such far-reaching and systematic reform had been ventured in England since the Age of Elizabeth."[42]

As already noted, none of these Commissions reported in time for legislation in 1832. Yet it must not be thought that Commissions of Inquiry had no influ-

[39] *Parliamentary Papers,* 1834, (No. 44) XXVII. This report was reprinted in 1906 (Cd. 2738).

[40] Edwin Chadwick. Bentham's proposals are to be found in his *Collected Works.* Part VIII.

[41] 4 & 5 William IV, c. 76.

[42] J. Redlich and Hirst, *Local Government in England* (1903), I, 108.

ence on legislation during that year of Reform victory. Previously established inquiries resulted in reforms in the system of courts (in particular that of Chancery) and in the reduction of the number of criminal offenses for which the punishment was death. On other topics, select committees of one or the other House of Parliament played their usual part; the most important parliamentary investigations of this kind being those on Irish resistance to the payment of tithes, slavery in the colonies, and the renewal of the charters of the Bank of England and of the East India Company.[43]

In the first year of the Reformed Parliament (1833) the Cabinet had to deal with a great outbreak of violence in Ireland. For this purpose the Grey Ministry introduced the Irish Coercion Bill, resisting the demand for inquiry on the ground that the evils were "so great and so notorious as to render inquiry superfluous."[44] But, though repressing the Irish disorders with especially vigorous action, the Ministry did not forget that the difficulties came from the existence of an Established Anglican Church in a Roman Catholic country. It was common knowledge that the riots in Ireland had grown out of resistance to tithe payments; and the Government undertook to solve this larger problem and at the same time to restore law and order in the country. On the larger issue, then, the Ministry relied upon the report of the Commis-

[43] The Bank of England charter was investigated by a "secret" committee. The slavery committee sprang from criticism of the Government's declared policy of ending negro servitude in the colonies; and, pending the report of the committee, the Ministry's program, as laid out by Order-in-Council, was suspended.

[44] *Annual Register*, 1833, p. 38.

sion appointed the previous year to investigate the ecclesiastical revenues of the Church in Ireland. Government bills were introduced for the purpose, among others, of reducing the number of bishoprics. Opposition to these measures came, it may be remarked, not only from the interested parties but also from Church supporters in England who feared this legislation as an incitement to similar action by nonconformists in England.

This year, 1833, saw the largest number of Commissions set on foot in one year up to this time. Yet of the 11 Commissions of Inquiry[45] two were semi-judicial in nature (to determine the claims of British citizens incurred during the wars thirty and forty years before, and to allocate among the colonial slave-owners the sums set aside by Parliament); three dealt with the same subject (municipal corporations), one for each of the three parts of the United Kingdom; and another was to consider for Ireland what was already being investigated for England (namely, the poor). The one major topic upon which a new Commission of Inquiry was immediately influential was child labor.

Few subjects were more bitterly controversial than the question of restriction of the employment of children in the rapidly expanding textile industries. The Grey Cabinet, it may be recalled, was backed by a majority of Reform Whigs and was opposed primarily by the Tories; but on many issues the Ministry

[45] Criminal Law Digest; Civilian Departments of the Army; Children in Factories; Scottish Court of Session; Municipal Corporations, England and Wales; Municipal Corporations, Ireland; Municipal Corporations, Scotland; Poor in Ireland; French and Danish Claims; Excise Department; Slavery Compensation.

felt the pressure of the less numerous Radicals, who looked to the enactment of a definite program of reduced taxation, cheap corn, lower hours of labor, and higher wages, as well as additional political reforms (such as the secret ballot, etc.). On the subject of factory legislation, the Government sought compromise. There had been numerous select committees in preceding years, most of which had done nothing but postpone action. Thus Sadler's bill of 1830 had perished in committee. In 1833 Lord Ashley (Sadler having failed of election to the new Parliament) introduced a similar measure for the regulation of children's employment in factories. It was "opposed by the great body of manufacturing capitalists, so many of whom had been sent into the House by the Reform Act, and who possess very powerful interests out of it."[46] The Ministry, though certainly not desirous of hurting the artisans, nevertheless sympathized with the manufacturers, whose support they needed. Supporters of the bill criticized select committee procedure on the ground that the members were partisan, prejudiced, and not completely informed by their very "selective" investigations;[47] and though the most ardent feared a Commission might be used "to procrastinate the bill,"[48] the motion for a Commission was carried, two members of the Ministry supporting it. Commissioners were sent to view the conditions in the mills, and, before the session ended, they reported that children were inadequately protected.

[46] *Annual Register*, 1833, p. 205.

[47] One member of a committee was reported to have remarked, "You had better let me make out my case before other evidence is gone into" (*ibid.*, p. 105).

[48] *Parliamentary Debates*, 3d series, Vol. XVI, p. 1001.

The Ministry, apparently fearing too drastic a measure, then attempted to have the bill sent to a select committee; but the Ashley measure was carried in Committee of the Whole by 164 votes to 141. The Grey Cabinet, having taken up the matter, now proceeded to put the bill through in an amended form—extending the number of hours to be worked and lowering the minimum ages. This ministry, it may be added, suffered a defeat over the date upon which the statute was to become operative but, not considering this a vital issue, did not resign.

Perhaps more important than the Factory Act has been the Municipal Corporations Act, which also proceeded from the investigations of Royal Commissioners. This was indeed the first great reform of city government since the Middle Ages, and its effects were both immediate and continuous throughout the rest of the century. It was well understood at the time that reform of the system of borough government must accompany parliamentary reform, for the "pocket borough" was but one aspect of the "close" corporation against which the newly enfranchised voters had long been protesting. A select committee of the House of Commons had previously reported "that corporations as now constituted, are not adapted to the present state of society." It had advised appointment of a Commission for further study, since the committee had been unable to accomplish a complete and impartial study owing to the methods of inquiry it used. They disapproved of local Commissioners of Inquiry, urging the need of a central body enabled "to command the evidence necessary to decide on the weight of conflicting statements." Such a body they thought should "in a short space of time collect the necessary information more easily and more accurately than it could be obtained by any other proceeding."[49] This was the procedure followed: three Commissions were appointed for England and Wales, Scotland, and Ireland, and special investigators were employed for the accumulation of information from all sections of the United Kingdom.

The results of the Municipal Corporations Inquiry resulted in legislation which is an important part of the constructive work for which the Reform Parliament is so famous. The careful nature of the investigation, conducted as it was by specialists (in so far as they existed at that time), has given an authority to the report which is shared only by the Poor Law report of the same period, a report which was likewise the product of careful research.[50] The clarity of the report has remained a model often emulated, but rarely attained, by later Commissions: "the Commissioners contrive to pack a concise but singularly lucid description of the general state of municipal institutions at that time and of the cause which had produced such a chaos of corruption."[51] The Municipal Corporations Act (1835)[52] which undertook to remedy these defects was significant not only because it extended political control to the new classes enfranchised by the Reform Act of 1832 but also because it

[49] *Annual Register*, 1933, p. 340 (where the report is printed).

[50] Cf. the discriminating praise bestowed on the methods of these two commissions by S. and B. Webb in numerous places, e.g., *Methods of Social Study* (1932), p. 156. The Report on Municipal Corporations is in *Parliamentary Papers*, Vol. XXIII, No. 116, 1835.

[51] Redlich and Hirst, *op. cit.*, I, 144.

[52] 5 & 6 William IV, c. 76.

set the pattern of local government for English boroughs for the ensuing century, basing the newly consolidated local governments on a rate-paying electorate with executive officers who were released from the ancient judicial connections.

The second year of the Reformed Parliament, 1834, found the Grey Cabinet, which had already experienced difficulties in conducting the Government, in a more precarious position than ever. The immensity and novelty of the reforming program upon which they were engaged made it inevitable that they should suffer as much from their nominal friends as from their avowed opponents. Though torn between the promptings of English Radicals and Irish Repealers and the hesitations of the potent industrialists, the Ministry had nevertheless invaded the field of factory legislation and was proceeding to attack the old poor laws and to make a clean sweep in the realm of local government comparable to that made in national institutions. The weakness of the Government lay in the fact that, though professing to carry out what would now be called a popular "mandate" for reform, they did not possess the support of a disciplined and united party. The attack of private members and the desertion of supporting groups was as damaging to the Ministry as the hostility of the official Opposition. Yet the Cabinet continued to stand behind its Commissions of Inquiry. At the opening of Parliament in 1834 the Speech from the Throne contained these words: "The Reports which I will order to be laid before you, from the Commissions appointed to inquire into the state of the municipal corporations, into the administration of the Poor

Laws, and into ecclesiastical revenues and patronage in England and Wales cannot fail to afford you much useful information, by which you will be able to judge of the nature and extent of any existing defects and abuses, and in what manner the necessary corrections may, in due season, be safely and beneficially applied."[53]

Strangely enough, however, the major difficulties which embarrassed the Grey Ministry did not come from these subjects upon which Commissions were already reporting. The dangers for the Government proceeded from the incompleted Irish questions. The Repealers led by O'Connell, not satisfied with the previous year's reduction of the Church establishment in Ireland, agitated for additional restrictive action, if not for complete disestablishment. A private member's motion for inquiry into the state of the Irish Church received such support that Grey found refuge in the appointment of a Royal Commission which was to investigate in each parish the needs of the Church in that country. Disunion was now revealed in the Cabinet, for upon the appointment of the Commission five ministers resigned. Nor did the schism within the Ministry end with this, for there was said to be a division of opinion over what to do with the surplus Church revenue which the new inquiry was expected to reveal. The inquiry had been opposed by O'Connell, on the ground that it was common knowledge that less than one-tenth of the Irish population was Protestant. The Opposition, led by

[53] *Annual Register*, 1834, p. 2. Only four new Commissions were appointed this year: Religious Instruction in Ireland; Post Office; County Rates; St. Helena.

Sir Robert Peel, also criticized the Government on the ground that the fullest information had already been procured, a claim which the divergent figures cited in debates in 1833 and 1834 sadly belies. In general, it seemed that the intentions of the Government were distrusted; the Opposition was divided between Peel's view that the inquiry was merely intended by the Ministry to postpone consideration of the matter for three or four years and the view of the more fearful that the investigation was quite definitely intended to precede spoilation of the Church and the confiscation of its surplus revenues. Would the Cabinet follow the report of the Commissioners? The several Ministers gave divergent replies. In the House of Lords, Brougham (Lord Chancellor) explained away the dangers: "It was to be purely a statistical inquiry,—one relating altogether to numbers and distances. Not one matter of opinion, or doctrine, or discipline, or observation, or remark, was to be embodied in the report, or be made any object of inquiry. If the chancellor of the exchequer (Althorp, leader of House of Commons) had said that the government would act on the report of the commissioners, he had said nothing more than that the government would act upon authentic information supplied to them by trustworthy and competent persons, and would feel itself bound, compelled, he might say, to recommend to the legislature such measures as might appear from the results of the inquiry, to be not only advisable but necessary."[54]

The end of the Grey Ministry, split over the Irish

[54] *Annual Register,* 1834, p. 64.

Church revenues, came shortly afterward. The occasion was another Irish question—the renewal of the Coercion Act of the previous year—and, after a defeat on this subject, the Cabinet resigned. But with the Reform majority in the House of Commons no Tory Ministry could survive. A reconstructed Whig Administration, under Melbourne, held office for a few months (during which time the Poor Law Amendment Act was passed and a bill to relieve the Jews of their disabilities was rejected by the Lords), until it was dismissed by the King in November 1834. Then Peel made an attempt to conduct the Government but was soon defeated in the next session (1835) on the old issue of the Irish Church revenues. Melbourne thereupon returned to office and, with a brief interruption in 1839 (the Peel "Bedchamber" episode), remained in power until 1841.

Having entered on a second life, the Reform Whig ministers continued their program. The Municipal Corporation Act was passed; but the Lords wrecked the Irish Church regulating bill, and it was not until the following year (1836) that tithe commutation laws were passed for both England and Ireland. Nine Commissions of Inquiry were appointed in 1835:[55] one of them to delimit the boundaries of the renovated boroughs, one of them to plan new Parliament Buildings made necessary by the fire, and one to do for Scotland what the religious census had done for Ireland. The year 1836 was likewise active with

[55] Established Church (revenues and duties) in England; Military Punishment; Pilotage; Municipal Boundaries; New Houses of Parliament; Religious Instruction in Scotland; Lower Canada Grievances; Irish Fisheries; River Shannon.

respect to inquiries; eight were appointed,[56] the most important immediate result being the requirement of registration of births, deaths, and marriages.

At last the Reform Parliament came to an end with the demise of the Crown and the accession of Queen Victoria in 1837. The great controversial reforms were now almost over, and the number of new Commissions of Inquiry fell proportionately.[57] Nevertheless, three great principles were enunciated in this closing period of reform: responsible government for the colonies (from Lord Durham's report on the Canadian rebellion); prepayment of postage (to become connected shortly with the penny postage); and the necessity for state intervention to protect adults as well as children in industry.

It is clear, from this review of the Commissions of the Reform Age, that in adopting the device of investigation prior to legislation, the Whig Reformers not only were accomplishing their ends in a day when expert administrators were first being trained and when an agreed party program had not yet been evolved but also were establishing a most influential precedent for the rest of the century. Never again did a determined group of leaders need to leave their policy to haphazard determination. Research and investigation had proved too valuable an aid to legislation, and had been too useful as a means of conciliating opponents and supporters alike, for this procedure subsequently to disappear. Yet the limita-

[56] Civil List, Heralds' College, etc.; Registration; Constabulary Force; Irish Railway; Aberdeen University; Glasgow University; Malta.

[57] In 1837, Unemployment among Hand-Loom Weavers, Irish Tithe-Owners' Relief, and Canadian Rebellion; in 1839, Roads; in 1840, Children in Mines, and Irish Grand Jury.

tions of the use of Commissions of Inquiry had also been clearly displayed: the reports of Commissioners must before all else be acceptable to the Ministry of the day; and the suggested lines of policy must appear reasonable to and in harmony with the political conscience of the politicians of the period. To the extent that the Reform Commissions had met these conditions, they had been successful; to the extent that they had not done so, they had failed.

STATUTORY COMMISSIONS

In general it may be said that two main political purposes are served by the appointment of Commissions of Inquiry: that of procuring information upon some major topic of political dispute; and that of conciliating public opinion. The two purposes cannot, of course, be clearly distinguished with respect to any single Commission. The establishment of an inquiry nearly always proceeds from mixed motives in which both the desire to have a current problem subjected to fresh and impartial analysis and the advisability of satisfying public demand for action are inevitably intertwined. The most that can be said of such investigations is that one or other of the motives seems to be dominant at the time the inquiry is set on foot.

The first of these purposes—procuring information—may present itself in a more or less automatic manner, as when a statutory requirement provides for the review of a given situation either at a definite time or under specifically determined circumstances. The best example of the latter type is to be found under the several Election Commissioners Acts since

1842.[58] When the election committee, which tried the disputed elections before 1869, or the judges who have tried them since that date, report corrupt or illegal practices, a joint address of both Houses of Parliament may secure the appointment of a Royal Commission of Inquiry. Thus in pursuance of the reports of such Commissions eight boroughs were disfranchised by statute in the years 1867 and 1870 (four in each year); and numerous individuals were temporarily or permanently disfranchised in 1870, 1871, and 1876. The last Commission under the statutory provisions was appointed in 1906 to investigate corruption in Worcester.[59]

The most noteworthy example of a Commission of Inquiry springing from such legislative anticipation is the Indian Statutory Commission of 1927. The appointment of this Commission was provided for in the reform of Indian Government in 1919. A new policy had been proclaimed by the Secretary of State for India on August 20, 1917, when it was announced that the British Government's intention was "that of the increasing association of Indians in every branch of the administration and the gradual development of self-governing institutions with a view to the progressive realisation of responsible government in India as an integral part of the British Empire." In accordance with such views, and more particularly in consequence of the Montagu-Chelmsford report,[60]

[58] May, *op. cit.*, p. 647. This authority cites first the act of 1852 and then the later ones (Note 2). There is no reference in any of the editions of Anson's *Law and Custom of the Constitution* to the part played by Election Commissions.

[59] *Report and Minutes of Evidence* (Cd. 3268–69, 1906).

[60] *Report on Indian Constitutional Reforms* (Cd. 9109, 1918). *Vide*, especially, pp. 5 and 277.

reform of the Indian Government was undertaken in 1919 when partial responsibility (dyarchy) was accorded in the provincial governments; and Mr. Montagu's declaration of 1917 was incorporated in the preamble of the Act as the "declared policy of Parliament"—with the proviso that the "time and manner of each advance can be determined only by Parliament."[61]

The statute had therefore provided for a review of Indian progress after ten years. In 1927 a Commission under the chairmanship of Sir John Simon was sent to India "for the purpose of inquiring into the working and system of government, the growth of education, and the development of representative institutions, in British India, and the matters connected therewith . . . ." They were to report "as to whether and to what extent it is desirable to establish the principle of responsible government, or to extend, modify, or restrict the degree of responsible government then existing therein, including the question whether the establishment of second chambers of the local legislatures is or is not desirable."[62] The Simon Commission, it may be admitted, was not well received by Indians, especially those of the Congress party, because there were no Indians upon the body. Connection with Indian opinion was attempted by means of a committee set up by the central legislature.

Both the strength and the weakness of the Commission procedure were well exemplified by the pro-

[61] 9 & 10 George V, c. 101.

[62] *Report of the Indian Statutory Commission* (Cmd. 3586, 1930), Vol. I, xiii.

cedure and reports of the Simon Commission and the final disposition of the Indian question. On the face of it, the Simon report was a monumental document. Probably never before had anybody undertaken an investigation upon which such a wealth of official and controversial literature existed. The report itself was a work of great wisdom and penetration. At the time of its publication, the Goverment had described it as a "document of enormous authority and intrinsic value, by far the most constructive contribution to the solution of the political situation in India that we have."[63] The first volume presented in masterly style a compact outline (such as was to be found nowhere else) of the historical, political, and sociological background of the Indian problem. The first printing of 10,000 copies was exhausted within two days; and a second printing of 28,000 copies was similarly sold out in a very short time. The appearance of the second volume, "Recommendations," was eagerly awaited. When published, it was perceived to tend toward conservatism; for while proposing the abolition of the system of "dyarchy" established in the provincial governments in 1919 and the substitution therefor of responsible government, the Commission regarded responsibility of the Central Executive to the Legislature as a matter for the more distant future.

The weakness of the Commission procedure was revealed when it became evident that the Government intended to treat the matter, if not as a political issue, at least as one not to be completely divorced

[63] Quoted in *Annual Register*, 1930, p. 53.

from political prejudices. Just prior to the issuance of the Commission's recommendations the Viceroy declared that the attainment of dominion status was implicit in the 1917 policy, and that the British Government proposed to summon a conference to which representatives from both British India and the Native States should be called to discuss a new constitution. The suggestion for such a conference had originated formally with the Simon Commission in 1929.[64] Meanwhile the Government had apparently taken fright at the response accorded to the Simon report, and had indicated that "a Report was, after all, only a Report."[65] Later it was explained that the Viceroy's statement had been intended not so much as a declaration of the Cabinet's intention to go beyond the report as to prepare for a good reception of the report by the public—and in particular the Indian public. The evident result was an indication that the report was not to be the basis for Government decision but was to be consigned to a very secondary place.

The first Round Table Conference was held in London in 1931, its opening and closing sessions being broadcast by radio throughout the entire world. To everyone's astonishment the Princes of India at once came forward with endorsement of the plan

[64] Sir John Simon wrote to the Prime Minister on October 16, 1929, to explain the need for enlarged jurisdiction which would enable them to consider a federation which would include the Native States. Mr. MacDonald replied that, having consulted the leaders of the other political parties, he welcomed the widened scope of the inquiry. Sir John had also suggested that, after reporting, the Government should meet the Indian representatives "for the purpose of seeking the greatest possible agreement for the final proposals which it would later be the duty of H.M. Government to submit to Parliament." (*Report, etc.*, I, xxii–xxiii.)

[65] *Annual Register*, 1930, p. 53.

for federation of all India which the Simon Commission had approved while regarding it as a rather remote possibility.[66] The Conservative party, taken somewhat aback by the unexpected success of Indian negotiation, now began to insist on the maintenance of certain "safeguards" in any new Indian constitution; and it was to these that the second and third Round Table conferences were largely devoted. Other problems meanwhile arose and failed of solution, especially the type of representation, whether territorial or communal; and even discussions in which Mahatma Gandhi participated as sole representative of the Congress party failed to resolve the difficulties.

In the meantime, important events in British politics had changed the entire political situation. The British Labour Government was succeeded in the autumn of 1931 by the National Government, dominated shortly afterward by the Conservatives. At the close of the year the status of the Overseas Dominions was firmly established by enactment of the Statute of Westminster; and at the Ottawa Economic Conference the following year there were revealed the economic antagonisms and rivalries of the growing nations forming the British Commonwealth of Nations. The British Government itself forsook (in peace time) the traditional free trade policy, adopting both "protective" measures and trade agreements. The new Government, though denying any change in policy, felt the necessity of meeting the parliamentary criticisms of the more conservative

[66] *Vide* also the (Butler) *Report* (Cmd. 3302, 1929).

members. And, since the Ministry was a "National" coalition, it was determined to leave the drafting of the Indian bill to a joint committee of the two Houses.[67] The result of this action, together with the amendments which were made in the various stages of the bill's passage through the two Houses, was the enactment of a statute of far more conservative type than might have resulted from the Labour Cabinet, but more liberal than would probably have come from a thoroughly Conservative Government.[68] The resultant Act[69] was therefore in no sense a product of the labors of the Statutory Commission, though it may be admitted that the final terminology permits a development which may be comparable to the system envisaged by the Simon report. There is no doubt that the report was a landmark in Indian constitutional evolution; there was no turning back, for it was impossible to accord less self-government than that contemplated by the Commission. The disputes revolved about the extent to which the report should be superseded by more radical proposals.

Three important subjects were treated in a political manner. There being no agreement among the

[67] No minutes of the proceedings of the joint committee have ever been published.

[68] The National Government was held to be bound by the Prime Minister's pledges that no change of policy would ensue; and the Conservative opponents of extensions of responsible government were voted down at the party conference in 1933 and 1934. The Secretary of State for India (Sir Samuel Hoare) pointed out that a large body of opinion which at first had favored a more gradual extension of self-government had been driven, as the result of "closer investigation," to the conclusion that "what was apparently the safer and wiser was really the foolish and dangerous course" (*The Times* [London], February 12, 1935). Mr. Churchill, the leader of the Conservative "die-hards," continued to recommend the adoption of the recommendations of the Simon report.

[69] 25 & 26 George V, c. 42.

Indians, communalism was extended to hitherto unexpected limits, special representation being accorded not only to the major religious minorities but also to women, and to commercial and industrial groups in some provinces. The promise of dominion status was not merely withheld, but only after great pressure was the preamble of the 1919 statute, respecting the attainment of self-government, withdrawn from the general repealing clause; i.e., it was not re-enacted, but it was not repealed as was the rest of the former Act. Lastly, the question of "safeguards" was so enlarged, both in the provinces and in the Federal Government, as to provide ample opportunity for the withdrawal of responsible government if necessary; and the result seems to amount to the introduction of dyarchy (in the matter of defense and foreign affairs) in the central government.

The history of the Government of India Act of 1935 indicates that today, as a century ago, the functions of a Royal Commission of Inquiry have changed very little. The first duty of an investigating body is to present reliable information upon a disputed subject. Then, in reporting its proposals, the Commission must not only provide a reasonable solution about which the ebb and flow of political controversy may center, but must also narrow within definable limits the area of such controversy. Experience with the Simon report shows that this is as true for a Royal Commission established under legislative pre-vision as it is for Commissions set up in the heat of political clashes. The honesty of the Commissioners and the wisdom of their proposals can be measured by the degree to which discussion and debate are focused on the specific suggestions they make.

THE GOVERNMENT'S USE OF INQUIRIES

It must not be expected that the close connection between politics and Royal Commissions of Inquiry which has been seen in the Reform Parliament of the 1830's should continue to be maintained to the same degree in later years. Since 1832 there has been only one complete and thoroughgoing change of policy comparable to that earlier transformation. The next occasion, that of the Liberal victory of 1906, was not, however, one as to which Royal Commissions occupied the same prominence that they had held early in the previous century. It is true that for a few years there occurred a noticeable increase in the number of new Commissions[70] (eight in 1906; two in 1907; seven in 1908; and six in 1909); but it will be observed that, while a number of these inquiries (such as those on Land Transfer, Welsh Church, Electoral Systems, Indian Decentralisation, etc.) were subjects dear to the radical Liberals, there were no investigations comparable in magnitude or importance to those of the Great Reform period. No Commissions were appointed to deal with the matters (such as Irish Home Rule, old-age pensions, unemployment-health insurance, or liquor trade, to say nothing of the budget provisions) for which the Liberal Ministry is most noted.

The use of Royal Commissions of Inquiry cannot

[70] *Vide* the list in Table IV, p. 194.

be regarded today as a substitute for Government policy. They may be utilized to advise upon new issues, neglected contemporary problems, or old and disputed topics; but they are not now usually invoked as aids in the enforcement of the Government's party program.

The influence of Commission inquiries upon legislation is generally too elusive for accurate determination. The most easily recognized cases of influence are those in which Government action follows, in a clearly defined manner, the results of the researches of a Commission. On such occasions the inquiries will probably have been resorted to by a Government seriously committed to the reformation of acknowledged abuses, or will have been undertaken by an indifferent Ministry which gives way to some form of pressure. Only rarely can the Government be expected to accept, with good or bad grace, suggestions for changes to which they are more or less definitely hostile.

The circumstances which lead a Ministry to appoint a Commission of Inquiry are as varied as the exigencies of political life. Roughly, however, they may be classified in the following manner, as inquiries: (1) to prepare the way for a predetermined Government policy; (2) to ascertain in a more or less "expert" fashion the best or most feasible solution of a problem the Government desires to tackle but on which it has made no final decision; (3) to shift to a representative body the task of solving some major economic or social controversy which the Cabinet does not feel called upon to settle; (4) to forestall public criticism or prevent anticipated political pressure; or, lastly, (5) to postpone as long as possible the consideration of a question distasteful to the Government of the day, and at the same time to pacify some politically powerful section of the public. It is needless to add that the decision to create a Commission may be the result of the joint operation of more than one of these considerations.

The occasions upon which the Cabinet places an inquiry in the hands of experts may be dismissed with a word or two. When technical skill is engaged from outside the official circles of the Government's advisers, it will often be found that the subject is one on which the Ministers have already made up their minds and simply need the Commission of Inquiry for its educational value or for the purpose of providing additional political ammunition in the parliamentary debates. Indeed, it has been asserted that the appointment of expert Commissioners rarely takes place without some admixture of politics. "The statesman who nominates the Commission can almost always determine the course it is going to take, since he will have a pretty good knowledge beforehand of the minds of the experts whom he puts on it, while, of course, avoiding any appearance of 'packing' his team."[71]

In other cases of "expert" inquiry it will be found that the Ministry and the special advisers are simply irresolute and afraid, owing to ignorance, internal divisions, or political timidity. In both types of case the appointment of an impartial or expert body of investigators usually provides a safe and acceptable

[71] W. Dibelius, *England* (1929), pp. 253–54.

way out of an unpleasant dilemma. The Commission bears the first brunt of criticism; and its report not only receives praise and blame from interested groups but serves as an indication of the strength of the respective contending forces. Then, after seeing both what is best and what is possible, the Government is able to bring forward a policy which has a very considerable chance of acceptance.

The Ministry of the day, it must be remembered, is increasingly pressed for time during the parliamentary session. Not only does the Government have to put through the usual routine business, such as the passage of the budget and the estimates, but the Cabinet is traditionally expected to propose at least one major piece of legislation each year.[72] In most cases this special legislative effort will be drawn from the political program of the party in power and cannot usually be left to the hazards of nonpartisan investigation. Any additional business, therefore, is a hindrance or at least a handicap to the already harassed Government. At the same time the Government cannot be deaf to the demands which are endorsed by sections of its own supporters; nor can it neglect the political agitations which excite the opposition parties or which indicate the existence of an influential opinion outside ordinary political lines. When certain social groups, economic interests, or powerful sections of the community are aroused upon some question — whether after long discussion, sudden awakening to an evil, or in consequence of a definite event or scandal—the Government has no alterna-

[72] W. R. Anson, *Law and Custom of the Constitution* (5th ed., 1922), I, 10.

tive but to appoint a Commission of Inquiry. The Government's intentions may vary from a serious desire to get to the bottom of a topic upon which the public is alarmed to the other extreme of hoping to "shelve" the question by apparently conciliatory action which will provide indefinite postponement.[73]

Examples of the use of Commission inquiries by a Ministry which has several definite purposes in mind have already been taken from the early years of the Reformed Parliament. Recent cases of a similar type can also be found. Generally speaking, however, these modern cases are of less significance than formerly; they tend to be confined to nonpolitical subjects which plainly require technical knowledge, and which are of public concern, but will probably involve a change of law hurtful to some interests. Under such circumstances it may be assumed that the purpose of the Government will be twofold: to provide the opportunity for an airing of a subject, and to enable the threat of public disapproval to be used against the objectors to the proposed remedies. The educational aspects, while not necessarily predominant, can undoubtedly be perceived in the inquiries in the first year of this century into arsenical poisoning and tuberculosis. Later inquiries into Coast Ero-

[73] This is an old procedure. Nearly a century ago J. T. Smith exclaimed: "How convenient it is to stop the mouth of any member of the House of Commons, if an inconvenient answer is asked, with the promising of a 'Commission of Inquiry' " (*op. cit.*, p. 178).

Disraeli was often charged with the practice of evading responsibility by referring embarrassing subjects to a Royal Commission or a select committee. *Vide* the cartoon in *Punch* (March 11, 1876) entitled "Civil Service Stores." "Dizzy" is at the counter with an obsequious shop assistant's manner: "What can we do for you, Madam?—Royal Commission? Select Committee? Papers? Careful consideration. Official Enquiry? Anything to oblige!"

sion (1906), Mining Subsidence (1923), Oxford and Cambridge Universities (1919), Dublin University (1920), Ancient Monuments (one each for England, Wales, and Scotland in 1908), Public Records (1910), Fine Arts (1924), Land Drainage, and National Museums (both 1927), all seem deeply tinged with the need of publicity prior to the expenditure of national money upon these matters or prior to legislation of novel nature.

But it is not only for the educative value in preparing the public for necessary changes that the various Governments have proceeded to set up Commissions of Inquiry. Occasionally party leaders have announced in election campaigns their intention to establish investigations. Thus Mr. Baldwin, in the 1924 election (having previously been defeated in 1923 on his campaign for protective tariffs which would not increase the cost of living), promised to set on foot an investigation into food prices.[74] In 1929 the strange situation was revealed of the leaders of the two major parties both promising an inquiry into the disputed, but nonpartisan, subject of licensing. Two Commissions were accordingly appointed by the MacDonald Ministry. No action followed the reports.

Frequently, it must be believed, the Ministry of the day has satisfied the demand for inquiry in the hope that the status quo will be endorsed in the report.

[74] His defeat in the 1923 election was agreed to have released the Conservative party from the protection program. It is noteworthy that when the National Government undertook the transition to protection in 1932—also promising to prevent noticeable rise of prices—it was carried into effect without either campaign pledges or Royal Commission Inquiry; as the result of imperial emergency it was accepted at the Ottawa Economic Conference of 1932.

Sometimes the agitation may be the result of the activities of cranks or of serious reformers. Examples of such inquiries are the Commissions upon Vivisection (1935), Divorce and Matrimonial Causes (1909), and Private Arms Manufacture (1935). Under these circumstances the Government may "pack" the Commission with respected and "uncommitted" men and women whose views can be relied upon as "safe." On occasions of this type, when the Government has no legislation to propose because it has no policy on the subject except one of inaction and hopes that no legislation will be necessary, the effect of such inquiries may be determined by the degree of unanimity revealed and on the ease with which the proposals for reform can be expected to pass the Houses of Parliament. But this must not be carried too far, for when the Government's policy is one of positive inaction the unanimity of the report can almost certainly have no effect. At the same time almost every Government is willing to take the credit for remedying an evil if the matter is largely noncontroversial and the solution is offered "ready-made." But on problems in which moral and religious prejudices are easily aroused and where the antagonisms cut across all party lines, the Government can rarely be expected to sponsor legislation which has no party backing and yet is intrinsically controversial. Public opinion, as is well recognized, has many "blind spots." It may refuse to recognize a clear social evil because it refuses to accept one of the definite alternatives of action which alone can offer relief. This has been shown consistently on the subject of divorce. Despite previous investigations, no amelioration of the palpably defective laws was acceptable until the public had reached the point where changes in law and procedure could be attained by a private member's bill (1936).

There have been numerous occasions upon which the Government establishes an investigation into a topic which has long been agitated and has at last reached a critical stage. Of these it may be said the Ministry's sole desire is, if not to forestall the popular demand, at least to mollify or pacify the public clamor for immediate action. In such cases careful manipulation of the terms of reference, as well as the advantage the Cabinet possesses of picking the Commissioners, is resorted to in order to save the Government embarrassment and to hinder the political consequences which might follow through investigation of the matter. In 1922, after considerable public criticism of the number of peerages and other honors distributed by the George ministries during and after the War, the Government set up a Commission, not to investigate the degree of truth in the allegations that peerages were frequently awarded for contributions to the party funds, but to propose remedies and a procedure for the future. No effort was made, as Mr. A. Henderson, one of the Commissioners, protested,[75] to interrogate the "touts" who were known to exist. The report of the Commission simply whitewashed the policy of preceding Governments, while deploring the possible evils which ensued from what was evidently regarded by most politicians (and by most of the Commissioners) as a

[75] *Report of Royal Commission on Honours* (Cmd. 1789, 1922), p. 13.

natural condition to be deplored but not changed. Yet two things did follow the inquiry: One was the establishment of Privy Council committee to pass on lists of honors to be presented to the King; each Prime Minister has appointed such a committee. The second was the passage of a statute imposing penalties for attempted solicitation of payments for titles of honor.[76]

The Arms Inquiry of 1935 may be regarded as a typical example of the use of Commission investigation for the purpose of evading criticism. In this instance, the direction of the inquiry was set, not by the terms of reference, which were unexceptionable, but by the personnel of the body. Nor did the Commission fail to justify the expectations of the Government that they would endorse in large degree the status quo.[77] The occasion of the appointment was the evident failure of attempts at world disarmament and the acknowledged policy of the Government in undertaking the rearmament of the British forces, as well as widespread interest in the United States Senate inquiry into a similar subject. The departure from the British disarmament policy of the preceding ten years provoked a renewed discussion of the private manufacture of armaments as to both the profit basis and the insidious influence of the arms industries in encouraging rearmament expenditures at home and abroad. The Commission reported, as was to be anticipated, against a state monopoly of

[76] There has been one prosecution under this act.

[77] It might perhaps be thought that the lack of compulsory power over witnesses hindered the inquiry; but it may be doubted if such powers, which were not requested by the Commission, would have produced any different result.

manufacture, which was the first question named in the reference.[78]

Quite frequently it happens that a Commission of Inquiry is utilized to appease an aroused public opinion (or even an anticipated popular outcry) following a notorious scandal or a specific example of executive incompetence, favoritism, maladministration, or illegal conduct. The circumstances out of which such inquiries have grown are, of course, quite varied and exceptional. A single event may precipitate a storm of criticism on a subject which has long been discussed but has hitherto failed to affect the public's imagination; one flagrant act of violence or of open disregard of the moral or legal conventions of society may drive a troubled people to demand drastic action. Such striking news as the landing of arms at Howth, a few miles outside Dublin, in 1914 produced such a sentiment, although the arming and drilling by unionist and separatist volunteers had been proceeding for months. A further example of more serious type can be drawn from the outbreak of the Easter Week Rebellion in 1916.[79] Similarly, discussion of the question of lunacy, with respect to both

[78] It must not be assumed from this that the report was in any sense an unreasonable one, or perhaps one not in accord with the best interests of all concerned. The point is that the Commission was appointed to mollify objectors to rearmament which might profit private manufacturers and its report thoroughly justified the Government's confidence in it. One does not need to guess what would have happened had the report been in the direction of radical innovation, as was the Sankey report on coal in 1919.

[79] The Commission absolved the Royal Irish Constabulary and the Dublin police from responsibility for the outbreak. "We are . . . . of the opinion that the Chief Secretary as the administrative head of Your Majesty's Government in Ireland is primarily responsible for the situation that was allowed to arise and the outbreak that occurred" (*Report of the Royal Commission on the Rebellion in Ireland* [Cd. 8279, 1916], p. 13).

"certification" and treatment, had been widespread after Dr. M. Lomax's book;[80] but the Harlett case may be regarded as the immediate occasion of the appointment of a Commission on Lunacy in 1924. Also, though the problem of postwar prostitution was disregarded, one phase of it, police interference with "accosting" in public parks, had been raised by Mr. Galsworthy's play, *Escape.* But not until the fifth or sixth of a series of much publicized cases, the Savidge case (involving a prominent ex-member of Parliament), did the popular outcry force investigation.[81] The Government, in difficulties of this type, may be moved by consideration of policy, for which the Cabinet may or may not be responsible but for which it will be held accountable, by a sincere desire to right a wrong, or by the need for removing the cause of a scandal or injustice which undermines public confidence in the administration.

The appointment of a Royal Commission is also a favored device for investigation of emergencies which suddenly confront the Government. The Cabinet may be at its wits' end because of the unexpected presentation of a critical problem which must be faced but on which neither the official experts are agreed nor the party program or policy is clear. And even when the Government is prepared to deal with

[80] M. Lomax, *The Experiences of an Asylum Doctor* (1921).

[81] Even then the question was not prostitution and accosting but the police procedure in interrogating witnesses and suspects. A Commons committee of inquiry pointed out the methods used in this particular case. The Commission on Police Powers and Procedure (1928) followed, for the purpose of ascertaining if the feared American "third degree" practices were in use among police departments. No legislation followed the report; but the high court judges made new rules respecting the methods of police questioning, and a new attitude of accosting was proclaimed for London.

the emergency it may suspect that it is incapable of overcoming the opposition which will be offered the remedies determined upon as necessary. Twice since the World War disputes in the collieries have led the Government to name a Royal Commission on the Coal Industry. It cannot be said that the Government either was taken unawares by the suddenness of the industrial struggle or was uninformed as to the issues at stake. Half a dozen Commissions and thirty parliamentary and departmental committees, to say nothing of twenty-six Acts of Parliament, had been concerned with the problems of coal production in the preceding three-quarters of a century. In each of the instances—1919 and 1925—the demands of the miners not only were a focal point of the political controversies of the day but had been debated unendingly in Parliament and in the press. Yet stoppage of production was bound to produce a national crisis of a most serious nature. The Sankey Commission (1919) was therefore appointed to ease the strain of threatened strikes; and although the Government refused to accept the permanent solutions offered in the later majority and minority reports, it did give effect to the most pressing remedies proposed by the majority (the chairman's) interim report by passing the Seven Hours Act and the Mining Industry Act (both 1920) as temporary expedients. Yet the coal industry remained in a disturbed condition, as the Government plans for district and national councils were rejected by the workers. A second threatened strike, in 1925, was met by the offer of a subsidy for the industry and the appointment of still another Commission. The Samuel Commission, it should be noted, differed from the Sankey body in being a small, nonrepresentative group of four persons unconnected with the industry. While not going to the extremes of two of the reports of the Sankey Commission which contemplated nationalization of the mines or national unification, the Samuel Commission did propose State purchase of royalties and the consolidation of the colliery operations. The report served merely to postpone the strike, which, when it occurred, was the occasion of the general strike of 1926. The Government introduced legislation carrying out many of the Samuel recommendations, such as the increase by one hour of the working day, and the provision of ameliorations of employment.[82]

The most recent example (1936) of an "emergency" being the occasion of an inquiry is the Arab revolt in Palestine, as a result of which a Royal Commission was sent to determine the causes and extent of the disorders. But here again there is no ground for considering the crisis one of unexpected occurrence. For fifteen years the successive British Governments have had before them the problems arising from Jewish immigration and the rehabilitation of Arab life in that country. Numerous other inquiries have been made, occasional disturbances have had to be suppressed, and the Colonial Secretaries and Cabinet have been in constant communication with both Arab and Jewish spokesmen. The Commissions on Malta (1931) and Newfoundland (1933) come within the same category. The political

[82] Coal Mines Act, Mining Industry Act, and others, 1926. No purchase of royalties was attempted, though levies upon royalties were imposed for pit-head baths, etc.

difficulties experienced with responsible government in Malta, whether or not due to Lord Strickland's inept manner, had been before the Government for some years. The suspension of the Maltese Constitution in 1930 cannot be regarded as provoking a crisis, though it did raise important problems, and the Commission which was established in 1931 may be considered not so much an inquiry into a crisis as it was a preparation for the restoration of the Constitution. The Newfoundland Commission, on the other hand, sprang directly from the request of that Dominion for aid in a time of extreme adversity. Yet even this case must have been capable of anticipation, for the inefficiency and corruption of Newfoundland politics were common knowledge long before.

PUBLIC OPINION AND THE GOVERNMENT

Very often, it is clear, pressure of opinion—which may be that of the general public, of the press, or of politicians—forces the Government to action which will to some degree satisfy the current demand while at the same time postponing the matter for later, probably much later, consideration. Commissions, in other words, are often established with the hope of "shelving" an issue which is thought to be of no urgency and which promises nothing but trouble for the Ministry. But despite all precautions, both as to the personnel of the Commission and the terms of reference, the Government sometimes finds itself faced with the necessity of making a decision.

An interesting example of this type occurred in 1935–36 over the problem of tithes. Exactly a century before, a statute[83] had authorized the cash commutation of tithes following the report of the Commission on Ecclesiastical Revenues. Despite uncertainties due to the relation of the amount to the current prices of the three main cereal crops, the collection continued in the hands of the individual tithe-owner (clergyman, cathedral, college, etc.) until 1925, when collection was placed in the charge of the Queen Anne's Bounty. A stabilized valuation was then placed on the hitherto variable tithe-rent charge. Successive ministers of agriculture in Conservative, Labour, and National Governments refused to consider for a moment any reopening of the subject.[84] Nevertheless the critical condition of agriculture in the worst years of the economic depression produced not only unsettled conditions but actual disorder. By 1933, while the Government still refused action, popular interference with the auction of property of farmers refusing to pay the tithe had become prevalent. At last the body of complaint had reached such proportions that the Government had to accept a change of policy. Early in 1934 the Minister of Agriculture (Major Elliott) announced his intention of introducing legislation and at the same time refused to appoint a Commission.[85] The compromise bill which was then introduced met such opposition from both tithe-owners and tithe-payers that the Government finally capitulated, and determined (June 13, 1934) to appoint a Commission. On eight occasions

[83] 6 & 7 William IV, c. 71 (1836). *Vide supra*, p. 101.

[84] In 1930 the Government even refused to receive a deputation on the matter. *House of Commons Debates*, 5th Series, Vol. 242, p. 698.

[85] *Ibid.*, Vol. 287, pp. 1621–22.

during the year 1935 efforts were made to draw an answer from the Minister respecting the expected date of the report and the action to be taken. When at last the Government did receive the report of the Commission, on December 5, 1935, it found itself in the peculiar position of being unable either to accept the recommendations of the Commission or to offer a substitute plan. For three months, an unprecedented period, the Ministry delayed both publication of the report and a statement of its intentions.[86] Finally, on February 27, 1936, both the report and the Government's white paper[87] were issued; and the Ministry introduced legislation to give effect to a variation of the settlement suggested by the Commission, a settlement which was finally carried through Parliament with amendment, though disapproved by nearly all parties to the controversy.

Cases in which the Government has disregarded the recommendations of a Commission have already been cited. There have been no cases in which the Cabinet has adopted a positive policy in direct opposition to the Commission's report unless, of course, refusal to follow the report is construed as pursuing an opposite policy. The Commissioners inquiring into any political controversy always realize the

[86] Mr. Baldwin admitted in answer to a question: "Reports of Royal Commissions have been published at varying intervals after they have been made, although I have not found any case where so long a period as three months has elapsed between completion and publication" (*House of Commons Debates*, 5th Series, Vol. 308, pp. 1780–81). (Had Mr. Baldwin's secretaries looked up *Parliamentary Papers*, Vol. XX, No. 301, 1826–27, they would have found many examples of delayed publication.) Annoyance in the House was considerable, especially after it became known that the report had been shown to the Archbishop of Canterbury. See also p. 190, and note 59.

[87] *Statement by H.M. Government* (Cmd. 5102).

trend of opinion and the possible lines that choice can follow; they have every reason to present recommendations which are capable of acceptance. There is, however, one significant instance in recent years of any inquiry precipitating a Cabinet crisis of more serious dimensions than the crisis of 1834. This is the crisis of 1931. The oft-told story does not need recapitulation here, except to recall that the Commission on Unemployment Insurance (1930) had recommended in its first report[88] that benefits be reduced and contributions increased in order to restore solvency to the insurance fund. The Labour Cabinet was unable to agree upon measures for reducing the expenditures, as urged by this Commission and other committees, and, faced by deadlock on its policy of economy and the danger to the gold supply, the Labour Government was replaced by the National Government. This new Cabinet, it may be added, carried out most of the recommendations of the reports in its Unemployment Insurance Acts and National Economy Act, 1931.

Finally, the use of Royal Commissions is not restricted in every case to the two types of situations wherein the Government seeks information or yields to the pressure of public opinion. The Royal Commission procedure is an executive weapon, and one may expect the Government to use these inquiries to its own best advantage. Many Ministries have done this to gain a good reception for their legislation. In other words, when the Government policy has already been decided on — whether it be part of the

[88] *Parliamentary Papers,* Cmd. 3872, 1931.

political program of the majority party or the result of administrative convenience or of technical necessity—Royal Commissions are often resorted to for their educative value. Though cynics may scoff at the statement, it does happen sometimes that Ministers are ahead of public opinion. Lawyers may realize that certain laws require reformation while the layman is still wary of legal change; churchmen may agree upon the modification of some forms and ceremonies or upon a revision of doctrinal interpretation when the mass of Church membership may think only in terms of Romanism and a dim recollection of the catechism; economic experts and Government advisers may perceive the trend of economic tendencies which are obscured from the sight of employer or worker, who see nothing but regimentation and state intervention; and statisticians and social workers may know the need for new forms of poor relief and housing long before the nation awakens to the problem. The Ministries of all political parties are thus subjected to incitement to progressive action by necessity, by pressure from their better-informed or more expert members, and by their department officials. If the Cabinet decides upon a policy when the public and the interested parties are not aware of its need, the most advisable course that can be pursued is the appointment of a Royal Commission of Inquiry. Not only does the naming of a Commission produce wide consideration and nonpartisan discussion of the matter in question, but the publicity given to the day-by-day proceedings of the Commission and the broadcast of evidence through the press serves to prepare the nation, consolidate support for the measure proposed, and diminish the effective resistance to the Government policy. Such a procedure is often adopted, therefore, when a change of long-accepted law is to be undertaken or when a novel departure in social policy is contemplated. In this respect it may be asserted that Royal Commissions serve not only the informational function which led the nineteenth-century Benthamites to adopt them but also the other great Benthamite principle of government, namely, publicity.

It should be unnecessary to repeat that Commissions can expect to have no more than an educational value if their recommendations are of such a nature as to be unacceptable to the Ministry of the day and incapable of being carried into law. The influence of the Reform Commissions of 1832 came not only from the importance of their subject matter and the novelty of their proposals but also from the fact the Commissioners and Ministers were to a large degree united by similar points of view. This condition of influence has remained true ever since then. When a late nineteenth-century commentator on the English Constitution declared that "policy investigation" was not a proper subject for Commissions of Inquiry,[89] he was either missing the whole point of the characteristic procedure of that century or was exaggerating the informing or research function in order to encourage the expert. A considerable number of the Commissions of Inquiry both in the nineteenth century and since that period have been appointed for the very purpose of considering controversial and

[89] A. Todd, *op. cit.*, II, 96.

disputed subjects. And the high reputation of this procedure has undoubtedly been gained by the success of the Commissions in achieving an acceptable report on issues over which partisan feeling ran high. For, after all is said about the relation of politics to Commission inquiries, the main functions of a Commission remain as ever: first, to get accurate and trustworthy information on a controversial matter; then, to agree upon the soundest, most politic, and most practicable policy to meet the situation which they have revealed. In doing this no Commission should divorce itself from the main current of contemporary political sentiment. The duty of the Commission is to act as a selective agency. It must assemble the pertinent and essential information; and, more important still, it must reduce the problems under consideration to such proportions that a wise choice is possible. The extent to which Commissions of Inquiry have succeeded in refining the questions they have investigated until they have been able to present a single acceptable solution is the measure of their success. No Commission has ever been able to determine policy; but every Royal Commission of Inquiry should take as its goal the presentation of such unchallengeable recommendations as will appeal to expert and politician alike as basically sound and practical.

LEGISLATIVE RESULTS OF RECENT COMMISSIONS

Just as there has been no Royal Commission of Inquiry into the Crown, so there has been no Royal Commission on Royal Commissions; but there has been an Inquiry by Commission into the exercise of some of the royal prerogatives (e.g., Honours, Army Appointments, etc.), and there has been a departmental committee on Royal Commission procedure.[90] Attention has already been devoted to the parliamentary interest in the number and cost of inquiries. The reason for neglect of the general subject of Commission inquiries is, of course, that each inquiry is undertaken in the belief that the object to be studied is a special case. Whether or not the report results in legislation depends upon certain political considerations; but after the issue is past no one cares to revive the topic.

It may be thought strange that while Parliament was highly critical and censorious in the matter of expenditures for Royal Commissions it should have raised no question as to value received. Rarely has the heretical doubt of the usefulness of the inquiry procedure been accorded official recognition. Yet only on two or three occasions has the advisability of knowing what results were attained by the inquiries been broached. In 1812, for instance, the Committee on Public Expenditures, "conceiving it highly expedient to examine from time to time into the benefit which either has been derived, or may be expected to accrue to the Public from the Commissions of Inquiry created by various Acts," called on certain of the then existing Commissions to report on their recommendations and the savings resulting therefrom.[91] After this, however, interest centered

[90] The case of a Royal Commission on a Royal Commission is to be found in one appointed in 1853 to consider "the Indian Law Commission's recommendations" (*Parliamentary Papers*, Vol. XXIII, No. 1, 1856).

[91] *Thirteenth Report* (No. 340, 1812), p. 3.

TABLE III

ROYAL COMMISSIONS AND THEIR RESULTS, 1921–1935

Year and Subject	Reason for Inquiry	Date of Report and Result
1921		
Importation of Store Cattle	Demand for end of 30-year-old embargo on Canadian cattle	1921. Advised admission; Government so acted, 1922.
Compensation for Damage by Enemy Action	To review claims and divide German reparations	1924. Awards; acted on.
Local Government of Greater London	Opposition to plan of London County Council	1923. A "split" report, rejecting L.C.C. plan; no alternative, no action.
Fire Brigades	To get national view of a local matter	1923. Suggestions followed by many local governments.
1922		
Honours	Long line of party-fund peerages, culminating in the Robinson case	1923. Government accepted the plan for review of Honours list by Privy Council committee, and statute penalizing offer to sell Honours.
1923		
Local Government	Local pressure for changes in charters, areas and functions	1926. Act of 1926 embodied in first report, Act of 1929 in later reports.
Superior Civil Services in India	Low pay a hindrance to recruitment	1924. Government largely accepted recommendations for pay increase
Mining Subsidence	Largest single cause of mining accidents	1927. Official objections caused rejection of report.

TABLE III—(*Continued*)

Year and Subject	Reason for Inquiry	Date of Report and Result
1924		
Fine Arts	Agitation for advisory body on civic betterment	1924. Continued as advisory body.
National Health Insurance	Medical objection to reduced panel fees	1926. Government carried through economies in contributions in accordance with report.
Lunacy and Mental Disorders	Hartlett case; agitation over certification and treatment	1926. Act of 1930 followed report.
Food Prices	Conservative election promise	1925. Only result was a Food Council.
1925		
Indian Currency	Fluctuations in the price of silver	1926. Report for stabilization accepted.
Coal Industry	Threatened strike	1926. Purchase of royalty rights not accepted.
1926		
Court of Session (Scotland)	Criticism of slow and costly procedure	1927. Report for shorter sessions and for jury changes.
Indian Agriculture	Depressed condition of rural population	1928. Provincial acceptance in varying degrees.
Cross-river Traffic in London	Criticism of the plan to tear down Waterloo Bridge	1926. Proposal for new bridges accepted.

TABLE III—(*Continued*)

Year and Subject	Reason for Inquiry	Date of Report and Result
1927		
National Museums	To prepare for coordination and for national subsidy	1930. Permanent commission appointed.
London Squares	Fear of encroachment on open spaces	1928. London following report as far as possible.
Land Drainage	Losses by winter floods; question of paying for efficient drainage	1927. Report followed by statute of 1930.
Indian Statutory	Provided for in Act of 1919	1930. Statute of 1935 after Round Table Conferences and Joint Committee drafting.
1928		
Police Powers	Savidge case investigated by Commons committee; fear of "third degree" methods	1929. Report followed by administrative and judicial changes in procedure.
1929		
Transport	Growth of road accidents	1930. Conference on report followed by statute.
Civil Service	Termination of cost of living bonus	1931. Report not acted on with respect to pension scheme.
Licensing (England) Licensing (Scotland)	Party endorsement of criticism of existing liquor regulation	1930. No result.
Labour in India	Industrial unrest and approach of political changes	1931. Negligible results followed recommendations for "amelioration of labour conditions."

TABLE III—(*Continued*)

Year and Subject	Reason for Inquiry	Date of Report and Result
1930		
Unemployment Insurance	Insolvency of the Fund	1931. Interim report rejected by Labour Cabinet; majority report (1932) accepted by National Government as to "means test."
1931		
Malta	Disturbed political conditions leading to suspension of responsible government	1932. Government accepted recommendation for restoration of the Constitution.
1932		
Lotteries and Betting	Widespread disregard of the law: Irish sweepstakes and dog-racing	1931. Interim report on totalisator accepted by the Government.
1933		
Newfoundland	Financial Insolvency	1934. Report recommending suspension of Dominion Status accepted.
Durham University	Intervention of the Newcastle City Council in Controversy over Medical College	1933. Government accepted report; Commission to reorganize the University.
1934		
Business at Common Law	Complaint at losses due delays in King's Bench Division	1936. Before report, the Lord Chancellor introduced a bill to enlarge the court.

TABLE III—(*Concluded*)

Year and Subject	Reason for Inquiry	Date of Report and Result
1935		
Arms Manufacture	Public concern at rearmament and sinister influences, profiteering	1936. Moderate report rejected by the Government.
Tithe	Government opposition to relief of farmers overcome by pressure	1936. Recommendations, somewhat changed financially, accepted by the Government.
Safety in Coal Mines	Accidents; question of adequacy of Act of 1911	
Tyneside Merthyr Tydfil	Most depressed areas in Britain, previously reported on by special officers, recommending further study	1935–36. Special aid and reorganization for reconstruction under national officers slowly accepted.

chiefly on costs. It was not until 1854 that a return was made of the legislative consequences of the efforts of various Law Commissions. It was ascertained that, following the reports of the Criminal Law Commission, eight statutes[92] had mitigated the old severity of capital punishment; but less benefit was found in the activities of the Criminal Law Digest Commission, to which only one statute, that respecting religious opinions,[93] could be attributed, two others having failed of passage.[94] Since that time, no such embarrassing questions have been asked.

[92] 1 Victoria, cc. 84–91.

[93] 9 & 10 Victoria, c. 59.

[94] *Return of the Number of Royal Commissions on Criminal Law*, No. 210, 1854–55.

In the absence of any official or unofficial analysis of the efficacy of Commission Inquiry, numerous beliefs have come into existence, such as that Commission reports rarely become translated into action until ten years later, that the same subjects of inquiry recur approximately every twenty years, etc. The desirability of an investigation of the quantitative and qualitative results of the inquiries of the past century cannot be doubted. A complete and comprehensive study of the subjects inquired into would prove a highly useful and informative work. Table III provides merely an outline of the Commissions appointed since 1921, with an abbreviated statement of the reasons for their establishment and the results following their reports.

CHAPTER V

PROCEDURE OF ROYAL COMMISSIONS OF INQUIRY

In choice of committees for ripening of business for the council, it is better to choose indifferent persons, than to make an indifferency by putting in those that are strong.—LORD BACON

WARRANT OF APPOINTMENT

Reference has previously been made to the ambiguities and inconsistencies which have sprung from misinterpretation of the term "commission" in constitutional documents of an earlier age. No such serious error can arise again. Yet, for the avoidance of less important ambiguities, it may be well to define the uses to which the term may properly be put.

In its widest sense "commission" is the act of entrusting authority to a second party. A "Royal Commission" is thus the conferring of power by the Crown upon individuals who thenceforth for its exercise become "Royal Commissioners." "Commissioners," said Sir Edward Coke, "are a delegation by warrant of an Act of Parliament or of the common law whereby jurisdiction, power and authority is conferred on others."[1] Accordingly, it is usually considered appropriate to apply the term "Royal Commission of Inquiry" to the following four aspects of the matter: (*a*) the royal act of delegating power; (*b*) the document by which this is accomplished;

[1] 3 *Institutes*, p. 165.

(*c*) the board or body of Royal Commissioners; and (*d*) this type of inquiry procedure.[2]

"This type of inquiry procedure" is the subject of the present chapter. Yet before entering into details it may be well to remove the frequent assumption that inquiry by Commission is but one form of inquiry by committee. Royal Commissions of Inquiry are quite different from committees of inquiry. They have, it is true, one important thing in common, namely, delegation of authority to a small body; and this common feature of very necessity produces some similarity in the process of inquiry, namely, the "conference" habit. But on purely formal or technical grounds it must be maintained that Commissions are not committees. A committee is a section or subdivision of a larger body to which the committee reports or is responsible. Thus the Continental "commissions" (as also the old Scottish Parliamentary "commissions") are really committees of the legislature. This is not true of Royal Commissions. A Royal Commission is no subordinate part of a larger body; it is in no sense a fraction or segment of Parliament, Courts, Privy Council, or Executive Departments. If a committee may be defined as a secondary organ of one of the institutions of the state, a Royal Commission must be defined not as such a secondary organ but as a primary institution, though of a temporary kind. In other words the Royal Commission is not created as a subordinate part of any other institution

[2] There is little need to add that the word "commission" has other meanings in other branches of government, e.g., in administrative law, in both England and America. In the latter country there is also a special meaning of "commission government" as a form of municipal organization.

but takes its formal origin from the legal center of authority, the Crown. When properly constituted a Commission is upon a formal equality with the other institutions of the state, such as the Courts, Houses of Parliament, Privy Council, etc.

Technically, therefore, the Commission form of inquiry involves the creation by the Crown of a new and transitory agency, which is not limited by convention or politics, by law or personnel, in the manner that subdivisions of the chief departments of the state would be. The census list of His Majesty's subjects alone limits the range of persons from whom Commissioners may be selected; they need be neither official nor elective, nor even partisan. The wisdom and experience of each Commission alone sets the bounds to the influence which its deliberations may exert upon public affairs. Each Commission that is appointed starts at scratch. No Royal Commission can rest on the laurels of a preceding Commission; each Commission's influence has to be earned and deserved. Its success is a personal one, though numerous outstanding successful Commissions confirm the belief in the advisability of retaining this "extraordinary" method of inquiry. Each noted failure will hinder the creation of other Commissions.

The occasions upon which the Royal Commission method of inquiry is resorted to and the motives which prompt this use have already been described. When the advisers of the Crown have once determined to establish a Commission, they do so by means of a document issuing from one of the departments of state. It makes little difference whether the authorization for such a Commission proceeds from a statute, from an address of one or both Houses of Parliament, or from ministerial initiative resting on the prerogative of the Crown.[3] Regardless of the political or legal origin of the inquiry, the nomination of the Commissioners and the statement of their powers is formally recorded in the "Commission," which varies little from case to case.

Several forms of appointment have been used. The rarest mode has been a Treasury "minute," i.e., a resolution of the Lords of the Treasury. Though often used in the nineteenth century, and in particular for Commissions authorized by statute,[4] this method of instituting an inquiry is more commonly confined today to the appointment of executive committees of an interdepartmental nature. Practically all modern Royal Commissions are constituted by letters patent, i.e., by a public document under the Great Seal, or by a warrant of appointment, a document attested by the Privy Seal or more rarely by the Sign Manual. Such documents may originate in any of the chief offices of state, though the majority

[3] Examples of Commissions arising from statutory provision are the Dardanelles and Mesopotamia inquiries (1916), the Sankey Coal Commission of 1919, and the Simon Indian Commission of 1927. Rarely does a Commission now spring from address of one or both Houses of Parliament. If the Cabinet is resisting an inquiry, the Opposition may bring the issue to vote on a motion for a Commission. In this case, the Ministers may feel it wise to accept the motion, as was done in 1922 when, after debates in both Houses over honors, the Government finally gave way before a motion in the House of Lords. Addresses of the Houses of Parliament are chiefly important now as being necessary either to bring about an election commission after report of corrupt practices (as in Worcester, 1906) or for the purpose of bringing a Commission already determined upon within the scope of the "contempt" powers of the Tribunals of Inquiry (Evidence) Act, 1921. This latter has been the case only once since the World War.

[4] An early example is the appointment of five Commissioners for the River Shannon investigation in 1835 (*Parliamentary Papers,* No. 61, 1836).

are said to proceed from the Home Office.[5] In the latter cases, once the decision to appoint a Commission is made and its personnel settled, the Home Office submits to the King the warrant naming the Commissioners and prescribing the terms of reference. But when so acting as the responsible Minister the Home Secretary's functions, we are told, are "little more than ministerial."[6]

The document, or warrant of appointment, which is the formal authority for the Royal Commission of Inquiry, falls in general into four parts: (1) salutation; (2) nomination of Commissioners; (3) terms of reference; and (4) date, place, and seal or signatures. At times there is inserted after the salutation an explanation of the reason for the appointment of the Commission, though the more usual form simply notes that "We have deemed it expedient that a Commission should examine . . . ."[7] The two most

[5] During a large portion of the nineteenth century it was customary to list the Commissions of Inquiry by the department issuing the authority for the purpose of returns made to the House of Commons. This practice seems to have originated in 1836 (Paper No. 528) when there were listed 22 Commissions from the Office of the Secretary of State, 2 from the Colonial Department, and 13 from the Irish departments (especially the Board of Works). It should be pointed out that these were not creations of that year but were Commissions then in existence.

[6] Sir Edward Troup, *The Home Office* (1925), p. 37. In 1834 the legality of the Irish Ecclesiastical Commission was attacked on the ground of its wrongful issue. At the end of April of that year four members of the Cabinet had resigned rather than approve of the Commission. Yet the Commission was issued on June 2, before their places were filled. The Duke of Wellington argued that the Commission could not have been authorized by either the Privy Council or the Lord Privy Seal. "The great objection to the commission was, that it had been made to proceed from the king, and not from either branch, or through the intervention of either branch of the legislature. It was the king who ordered that the great seal should be put to the commission . . . ." The opposition accordingly viewed this as a most dangerous precedent. Yet the evident disregard paid their arguments by the government indicates that it was fairly insignificant. *Vide Annual Register,* 1834, p. 64.

[7] Cf. the typical Commissions in the Appendix. Note in particular that in the Newfoundland Commission of 1933, since the future of a

important parts are of course those naming the Commissioners and declaring their duties. The names of the Royal Commissioners are set down in order of official precedence, commencing with the chairman, who is often a Privy Councilor. Great care is exercised in the brief statement of the subject of inquiry, for this is the occasion of the Commission's issuance, and when the labors therein noted are completed and the last report presented the delegation of authority will come to an end.

There is rarely any indication of a time limit upon the inquiry. Political necessities find no reflection in the wording of the Commission. Appointments, however, are not for life, nor even during good behavior, but are intended to be effective while the investigation is being conducted. Death or resignation of members may necessitate additional appointments by royal warrant or by letters patent. Where no new appointments are made to fill the vacancies which arise in the course of extended researches, the Commission may be considered defunct if no report is made after the lapse of months. Vacancies in membership, the desire to increase the numbers, or the determination to change the chairman (or First Commissioner) may be the occasion for the issuance of a new Commission superseding the former.[8] Only one

---

Dominion was at stake, the Commission definitely declares it is issued "on the advice of Our Ministers in Our United Kingdom of Great Britain and Northern Ireland, in Our Dominion of Canada and in Our Island of Newfoundland . . . ." There is no other case of a Commission issuing on the advice of three different Cabinets.

[8] Examples may be found in *Parliamentary Papers,* LXVI, No. 342, 1887. Todd cites dismissal of a Commissioner by the issuance of a new Commission from which his name was omitted (*Parliamentary Govern-*

case has been noticed of a Commission being self-perpetuating: the Commissioners appointed to advise on the site for the new Law Courts in 1865 added eighteen new members in 1870.[9]

Royal Commissions continue in existence until the completion of their labors or until superseded by a new Commission. The life of a Commission may thus expire after a few months or may extend over a score of years, as has the Commission on Historical Manuscripts, first constituted in 1869 and still publishing reports. The demise of the Crown has at times resulted in the reissue of numerous Commissions, as in 1830 and 1837. But by the time of the death of Queen Victoria steps had been taken against the legal consequences of the change in the person of the ruler. The common-law doctrine that all offices held under the Crown determined at its demise was finally abrogated and negatived by the Demise of the Crown Act, 1901.[10] Nevertheless, upon the accession of George V the issuance of the first Royal Commission by the new monarch was taken as an opportunity to validate the continued existence of some eighteen Royal Commissions of Inquiry.[11] There is no case of a Royal Commission being discharged prior to the completion of its duties.

ment in England [Walpole, ed., 1892], II, 101). No recent example of this kind can be found.

[9] *Parliamentary Papers*, LXXXI, No. 426, 1888, p. 4.

[10] 1 Edward VII, c. 5.

[11] George V's accession was on May 6, 1910; on May 30, 1910, was issued the warrant for the Commission on Divorce and Matrimonial Causes. This warrant explains that the Commissions (which are then listed) were "still engaged upon the business entrusted to them" at the late demise of the Crown and are therefore authorized to continue their labors as if under commission from His present Majesty. *Parliamentary Papers*, XVIII, Cd. 6478, 1912–13, pp. iv–v.

PERSONNEL

The manner in which the Commission is constituted depends upon the purpose to be served by its creation. The type of members thus varies with the nature of the political intentions which led to the adoption of the inquiry. If the Government has in mind simply the satisfying of a public demand for investigation of a current problem, it is clear that the choice of distinguished nonentities will serve just as well as the selection of the most experienced and capable persons available. If, on the other hand, the Government resorts to a Commission of Inquiry because it is in a dilemma between two lines of conduct, it will take care to seat on the Commission men whose practical sagacity in seeking a compromise will carry weight with the interested public. When it is remembered that there have usually been between ten and twenty Royal Commissions functioning at any given time, it may be a matter for some astonishment that the Government can always find a sufficient number of important and influential persons who are willing to serve in an unpaid capacity upon a body which will have many lengthy and perhaps dreary public sessions, numerous wrangles, and finally have to labor over voluminous reports and papers. Yet there never has been any difficulty in securing the most eminent and the busiest men for the more important Commissions. Fortunately, membership on a Royal Commission has been regarded as an honorable and desirable testimonial of distinction in politics, business, or scholarship. In addition to those whose public spirit involves occupying themselves in such matters, many persons are eager to serve because their interests are at stake in any economic or social change. The publicity, recognition, and influence which are accorded Royal Commissioners undoubtedly keep up the supply of those willing and anxious to undertake these advisory duties.

There is, perhaps, an oversupply of volunteers for Commission and committee service. Provincial jealousy has been shown at the supposed favoritism which is believed to be shown to residents of the metropolis. In 1933 the Home Secretary (Mr. Hore-Belisha) was persuaded to declare that "in selecting personnel all relevant considerations, including territorial considerations where appropriate, will be borne in mind, the objective in each case being the appointment of a committee [the question raised being committees as well as Royal Commissions] composed so as to promise the very best possible guidance on the subject referred to."[12] Very frequently, it may be remarked, the personnel of specific Commissions has been the subject of debate in the Houses of Parliament.[13]

The size of Royal Commissions has extended from one single Commissioner, as in the case of Lord Durham's appointment for the investigation into difficulties in Canada (1837), to twenty-one members, in the English Liquor Licensing inquiry (1929).[14] The num-

[12] Mr. Rhys Davis had asked in the House of Commons on February 13, 1933, as to the distribution of members of Commissions appointed by the Cabinet. *House of Commons Debates*, 5th Series, Vol. 274, pp. 1032–33.

[13] In addition to the older references cited by Todd (*Parliamentary Government*, II, 97), cf. *House of Commons Debates*, 5th Series, Vol. 274, p. 1032; Vol. 290, p. 1691; Vol. 291, pp. 542, 1560, 2086. On the personnel of the Simon Commission, *vide Annual Register*, 1927, pp. 108–10.

[14] Two Commissioners sat on the inquiries into special areas (Merthyr Tydfil and Tyneside, 1935), three Commissioners on the Irish Re-

ber of Commissioners is chiefly determined by the type of Commission, i.e., whether expert, representative, or impartial. Generally speaking the representative Commissions are the largest, for it is understood that members are often selected not only on merit but on their being acceptable spokesmen for special interests. Thus what is probably the most important representative Commission of this century, that on the Coal Industry (1919), consisted of men practically designated by the contesting parties: three coal-owners were named by the Mining Association; three union officials were named by the Miner's Federation; and the Federation suggested also the three economists (members of the Fabian Society), who were to counterbalance the three "capitalists" nominated by the Government as representing the chief industries dependent on cheap coal.[15] The thirteenth member, the chairman, was a distinguished judge of "liberal" views, Mr. Justice Sankey. Among recent Commissions, the largest have undoubtedly been the Licensing Commissions, of which the English body consisted of twenty-one members, distributed as follows: trade unions, 4; temperance societies, 3; liquor interests, 3; business men, 2; cooperative societies, 2; social workers, 2; government experts on licensing, 2; and the secretary of workingmen's clubs, a woman from local government bodies, and a chairman unconnected with the matter.

The large representative Commission has probably

---

bellion (1916), four Commissioners on the Coal Industry (1925) and on Unemployment Insurance (1930), etc.

[15] S. and B. Webb, *History of Trade Unionism* (rev. ed., 1920), p. 518.

been more criticized than any other type. Its defects are patent. Such a body is unwieldy; and its hearings are more likely to turn into partisan debates between Commissioners who regard themselves as counsel for their respective sides. The elementary concept of an "inquiry" is thus lost; the purpose becomes one of getting a "case" recorded as favorably as possible. As there is little co-operative effort under these circumstances, there is little corporate wisdom; the conclusions of the Commissioners are embodied in majority and minority or dissenting reports, which merely perpetuate the original cleavages in the Commission. These objections to the representative Commission were perceived by the Balfour Committee on Royal Commission Procedure in 1910: "It seems to us impossible to avoid the conclusion that appointments have sometimes been made to Commissions of individuals whose proper place would rather have been in the witness box than on the tribunal. A Commission selected on the principle of representing various interests starts with a serious handicap against the probability of harmony in its work, and perhaps even of a practical result from its labours." "We are also of opinion," the committee proceeds, "that there has been a recent tendency to make the membership of Commissions too large. The object in view is probably to ensure that various shades of opinion should be represented within the Commission, a consideration to which we attach little weight."[16]

Yet no heed has been paid to this protest. A great many of the postwar Commissions have been large

[16] *Balfour Report,* p. 6.

and have been representative in character. Indeed, it has been urged that the very nature of democratic government requires that Commissions of Inquiry should be representative; for "once it has been admitted that government is only by the consent of the governed, the representation of interests upon the Commissions is an unavoidable conclusion."[17] Nor is it felt by those who argue in this manner that the tendency of representative Commissions to produce a multiplicity of divergent reports is bad in itself. On the contrary, the view is advanced that the very fact of recording the opposing views—say, on the subject of nationalization of coal mines—in majority and minority reports serves the major purpose of an inquiry, i.e., bringing into the public eye the evidence and arguments of both sides, especially since one of these may have been entirely suppressed or disregarded previously. But the proper reply to this is that the place for the expression of partisan arguments is the legislature, and the persons best qualified to engage in this controversy are the party spokesmen.

There is more to be said on behalf of representative Commissions which produce a unanimous report. The solutions offered by the Commissioners in such a case may not be theoretically sound, and in principle they may be condemned by all parties; yet the very fact that the report issues from a representative Commission which could reach a considerable body of agreement on controverted matters is itself a useful indication that accord can be attained. More-

[17] H. Finer, *Theory and Practice of Modern Government* (1932), II, 756.

over, such a report shows the lines of possible peaceful solution. Whatever may be said against compromising concessions in such reports as destructive of public honesty and sound policy, it remains true that unanimous reports, regardless of the soundness of their technical basis, undoubtedly carry greater weight with Parliament and with the public generally than the best-intentioned set of minority reports.

The Balfour Committee quite properly considered that every effort should be made to ensure unanimity and, if this were not possible, that the dissident opinions should appear not in the form of a formal minority report but as a memorandum of dissenting notes. The "report" should be work of the Commission as a whole, and exceptions to special parts should be allowed dissentient Commissioners at the end. This seems indeed to be highly desirable in a Commission of Inquiry. Certainly all members of the body should agree upon the factual evidence and upon the state of law and administration on the topic being investigated. Divergence of opinion as to explanations of the existing situation and the type of remedies to be adopted might properly exist and in this case find their statement after the opinions of the majority have been formally recorded. This is the usual practice with respect to the form of reports of Royal Commissions. One report is presented, with occasional notes at the end indicating special disapproval of one section or another by one or more Commissioners. And when such a form is followed the report is far more influential than a multiplicity of reports. Where a representative Commission does produce one or more reports, the situation is aggravated if there is a political basis for the division, as for example the division in the Labour Commission in 1893, when the minority report became a party pamphlet of the Independent Labour party. The same might be said of the reports of the Sankey Coal Commission of 1919.

Representative Commissions are often a failure because they fail to be truly representative. They suffer from the same defect which has vitiated national economic councils: the impossibility of determining representation which will satisfy all the interested parties and at the same time indicate the proper balance among social forces. On questions which involve employment and industrial relations it is customary to assign to the various interests an equal number of already predisposed experts. The entire Commission is staffed not so much to represent all interests as to checkmate the chief contenders in an industrial dispute. Responsibility for breaking the deadlock is thus thrust primarily upon the chairman, whose vote is necessary to produce a majority upon any question.

Moreover, not all representative Commissions are representative of the public interests concerned. Many Commissions consist of politicians drawn from the political parties in the Houses of Parliament. In 1922 the Commission on Honours represented the hereditary peerage and the elected members of the Commons parties. There was no direct representation of the electoral-party organizations, of the parliamentary machinery of the dominant party, of the new "creations," or, of course, of the public. So too the Simon Commission on India—which, though a statutory Commission, did not have to consist of members of Parliament[18]—contained no spokesmen for either British Indian or Native State interests.

There is every reason for believing that representative Commissions are not the best bodies for engaging in the "inquiry" procedure. The task of hammering out a politic compromise or practical solution when rival views are held by organized and entrenched interests can most effectively be accomplished by joint committees of the Houses of Parliament or by political and industrial conferences which are openly instituted not for "inquiry" but for "discussion." "The true object of the appointment of a Royal Commission is to obtain a carefully considered judgment in the matters within the terms of reference; and this object is imperilled when the preliminary considerations mentioned above [referring to representation of interests] are disregarded, because its members are apt to divide almost from the date of this appointment into two or more opposing parties."[19]

The most admirable results have been obtained from Royal Commissions composed of expert or impartial persons. There are two requisites for the successful conduct of an inquiry. There must first be a

[18] It was frequently asserted in defense of the exclusion of Indians that since the Commission was responsible to Parliament, it must be constituted solely by parliamentarians! The nonsense involved in this widely accepted view is revealed by the recalling of the composition—in fact, the nomination—of the Sankey Statutory Coal Commission in 1919. Commissions only inquire and report; it is the Cabinet which is responsible to Parliament for the determination of Government policy. Statutory Commissions have no more responsibility to Parliament than other Commissions.

[19] *Balfour Report*, p. 6.

thorough and disinterested investigation of the facts pertinent to the subject. Secondly, and even more important, is the mature interpretation of the evidence with a view to the determination of a mode of future treatment of the subject at issue. These two things, patient investigation and unprejudiced weighing of causes and effects, which may be called research and judgment, are best undertaken by experts or nonpartisans.

Expert Commissions, i.e., those manned by persons whose special competence in the subject of the inquiry or in related fields is recognized, have been used quite frequently for advisory purposes in such technical matters as public health, local government administration, and other problems in which professional competence is an admitted asset. The chief advantage of this kind of inquiry is that the issue is removed from the arena of political debate and subjected to scrutiny by influential authorities who have no personal concern or commitment of party affiliation. It provides an opportunity for utilizing the services of specialists who are not normally members of legislative bodies and who do not happen to possess official connection with the administrative departments. Being already prepared and trained, specialist Commissioners do not have to undergo the "educative" work which so frequently forms the first part of the work of inexpert Commissions. From the very outset the Commissioners bring to the investigation a body of information and experience which enables them to proceed immediately to the heart of the matter, to sifting out indisputable facts, weighing the various interpretations which are offered in explanation of social phenomena, and attempting to arrive at a mature, collective judgment.

Even more valuable than expert Commissions are "impartial" Commissions; for the latter are capable of much wider use and are of greater applicability in the less exact sciences of social life. On these bodies, the members may be eminent parliamentarians, distinguished publicists, or trustworthy persons from any walk of life. There is, in fact, no such limit to the area of choice for such persons as there is in the case of experts and representatives of special interests. There are, indeed, two principles upon which selection must be made: First, that whatever the members' affiliation, aptitudes, or avocations, they must be men whose integrity and impartiality cannot be impugned. Second, that they be men whose reputation for sound judgment is such as to give their recommendations considerable weight with Cabinet, Parliament, and the public.

It will be objected, of course, that in bitterly controversial issues, or in all disputes where vested interests are affected, impartial Commissions are an impossibility. Thus the Webbs have remarked: "When we are told that a particular person has been appointed on a Royal Commission or Government Committee . . . . on the ground that he is or claims to be an 'impartial party,' we may rest assured that this means merely that the selector and the selected *agree in their bias*."[20] Even when a serious effort is made to select men who have every appearance of impartiality, it is sometimes difficult to secure promi-

[20] S. and B. Webb, *Methods of Social Study* (1932), p. 45.

nent individuals who have not expressed themselves upon a current controversy—as Mr. Baldwin explained in excusing the tardiness of appointments to the Arms Inquiry in 1935.

Moreover, as appears from the review of the relations of Commissions to politics in the preceding chapter, it may be objected that what a Government wants in a Commission report is not a "sound" judgment but an "acceptable" one. On all questions of policy the final decision rests in the hands of politicians, whose determination will often be dictated by political considerations which bear little or no relation to expertness or impartiality. Thus, it may be recalled that in 1919 the "representative" Sankey Commission on the Coal Industry was without influence because of the multiplicity of its reports and the "impartial" Samuel Commission of 1925 on the same subject was likewise disregarded despite its unanimous recommendations of a serious nature for permanent solution of the problems of the coal industry. In both cases conservative or vested interests nullified the results of compromise among the majority Commissioners in the first case and of the unanimous disinterested Commissioners in the second.

Yet this criticism must not be pushed too far. There are certain issues in modern politics upon which it is evident that not knowledge (or "truth") but will (or "interest") is decisive. It is not necessarily the function of Royal Commissions of Inquiry to solve these political disputes, though the occasional success of a representative Commission in this direction is all to the good. The function of the Commission of Inquiry is to formulate the essential phases of special knowledge and technical information so as to permit the "willful" political choice to be made not blindly but with full recognition of the factors which are involved. It has never been the duty of investigative bodies to determine policy; their task is to narrow a field of contest, to bring the disputants to an "issue," and to suggest a "most approved" choice.

The demand for representation on Commissions and the distrust of experts have sprung very largely from a disbelief in the impartiality of appointees, whether expert or not. Thus in 1903, the trade-union leaders, justifiably incensed at the legal consequences of the Taff Vale decision and convinced of the prejudices of the entire legal profession, refused to testify before the Commission on Trade Unions, which was a nonrepresentative body of lawyers. More recently still it is clear that, without any reflection being cast upon the probity of the Commissioners in the case, the influence of the report of the Arms Commission was weakened by the revelation in the course of the proceedings that the Chairman was, unwittingly, a shareholder profiting from the munitions production through the Imperial Chemical Industries.

The experts, too, it is frequently urged, are not open-minded; they come to the inquiry with prejudices proportionate to their degree of expertness and frequently tend to disregard or discredit new evidence and contrary opinions to such an extent that it has been suggested they could as well have prepared the report prior to holding the hearings. Yet the need for utilizing experts is so imperative that they, or at least openly partisan "experts," are always placed upon the representative Commissions.

as well as upon impartial and expert bodies.[21] "The report of a Royal Commission," it may be affirmed, "is valuable in proportion as it expresses the agreement of competent minds upon the various factors of any problem arrived at after full and unbiased inquiry; its value rises in proportion to the extent to which its unanimous recommendations cover the whole field. It affords little help towards administrative progress if the evidence brought before it is utilised merely to confirm prepossessions, to bolster up opinions, to support interests."[22]

In conclusion it may be said that it has been the admirable nature of the personnel of Royal Commissions in the past which has contributed more than anything else to the satisfactory results obtained from the Commission system of inquiry. Whether the members have been expert or biased, representative or impartial, it can rarely be said that they were incompetent or negligent. Whenever the Government of the day has really sought elucidation of a subject, it has received a carefully considered study of the matter. For the members of these Commissions are not only men of position and influence; they are earnest investigators, who take their duties seriously. The work is seldom delegated to subordinates—indeed, it might be more frequently than it is—but is undertaken personally at considerable sacrifice of

[21] The Parliamentary Science Committee, in a letter to the Prime Minister dated May 8, 1934, urged the desirability of including scientists and technicians upon all commissions and committees dealing with scientific and technical matters. On the last day of that month, no answer having been received, a question was asked in the House of Commons; in reply to it, Mr. Baldwin refused to commit himself to a promise: "I think it would be inadvisable to lay down any general rule" (*House of Commons Debates*, 5th Series, Vol. 290, p. 354).

[22] *Balfour Report*, p. 7.

leisure, earnings, and even social reputation. But whether from being clever politicians, unquestioned specialists, or sincerely disinterested persons, the fact is that a number of reports have carried sufficient weight to influence policy in the long run; and this has been so continuous that the use of the Royal Commissions has been regarded as a certain and satisfactory way out of all manner of difficulties.

VARIABLE PROCEDURE

There is an almost infinite variety in the methods and procedure employed by the various Royal Commissions. For, in addition to the differences of subject matter which are dealt with by the individual Commissions, these bodies are special creations, the life of each of which expires after its final report on the particular topic it investigates. Both the common body of information, except as embalmed in the report and evidence, and the membership which has just become accustomed to joint work are dispersed to the four winds, with no prospect of reassembly on this or a similar matter. There is little chance, therefore, for the development of a continuous body of precedents as to the manner of proceeding except as some individual member may have participated in previous inquiries. It was for this reason that the Balfour committee on Royal Commission procedure gave up the attempt to establish a code of rules and confined itself to proposing that a circular of recommendations be sent to each Commission as appointed.[23]

[23] "The circumstances of Commissions are so variable, and the difficulties so difficult to forsee, that we are unable to recommend the prepa-

The specific problems of procedure which will arise will be dependent upon the subject of the inquiry and the nature of the personnel of the Commission. The definition of the purpose of the inquiry will of course be found in the terms of reference in the document instituting the investigation. Great care is usually taken in drafting the statement of the topic to be studied. But the reason for the inquiry is rarely mentioned; and though this is generally a matter of common knowledge, there frequently arise misunderstandings or differences of opinion as to the interpretation of the Reference. It has long been regarded as important that the department which was responsible for the establishment of the Commission should be prepared to interpret in a practical way the subject upon which they require information.[24] On the face of it the widening and narrowing of the subject is ostensibly in the hands of the Government for whose benefit the inquiry is being conducted. For this purpose additional instructions may be sent to the Commissioners, and it is the practice for the chairman to consult the appropriate persons before entering upon the study. Yet it is the Commission which has to wrestle with the subject, and they may accept or not the department recommendation.[25] On occasion the Commissioners, even when appointed

---

ration of a code of rules such as has been suggested" (*Balfour Report*, p. 3). The draft circular which embodied most of the committee's recommendations is at p. 5 of the *Report*.

[24] J. Hatsell, *Precedents of Proceedings in the House of Commons* (ed. of 1818), IV, 70–113.

[25] Advice usually is sought from the Home Office, but it has absolutely no power of giving an authoritative decision (*Balfour Report*, p. 9). An early example of the need for elucidation of the functions is provided by the correspondence between Lord Althorp and the Poor Law Commission in 1833 (*Parliamentary Papers*, No. 71, 1833).

under statute, may request an enlargement of their Reference in order to include a wider view of the matter in hand, as did the Simon Commission on Indian Affairs in 1927.[26] But, in any case, as the body which is actually to perform the work of investigation the Commissioners will be able to perform their duty only in so far as they understand it or are agreed upon the purpose.

When agreement is reached on the extent of the inquiry the next question is the method of conducting the investigation. The type of Commission, as expert, impartial, or representative, will likewise influence the method to be used. Expert and impartial Commissions will be more likely to commence with individual study of the problem before holding hearings; representative Commissions will probably utilize specialists for the purpose of investigation of specific problems, while proceeding with public sessions, provided the subject matter lends itself to this treatment. The procedure will thus depend both upon the subject matter and the composition of the Commission.

The most unusual procedure has been that of the "secret" Commission. Only two of these were established in the nineteenth century, and both were concerned essentially with the same subject, the conduct of the Princess of Wales in the first years of the century. The reasons for secrecy can easily be understood, though it might be admitted that this was a bad procedure.[27] The first Commission was ap-

[20] *Vide supra*, p. 118, note 64.

[27] In 1820, when the Prince of Wales had succeeded his father as King George IV, the return of Princess Caroline to England of necessity

pointed in 1806 to investigate the truth of certain charges respecting the conduct of Princess Caroline.[28] A Royal Commission under the sign manual instructed Lord Erskine (Lord Chancellor), Lord Spencer (Secretary of State), Lord Grenville (First Lord of the Treasury), and Lord Ellenborough (Chief Justice) to conduct the "delicate investigation," as it was called. The four Commissioners, with Sir Samuel Romilly (Attorney General) acting as Secretary, pursued the inquiry in secret, without summoning the Princess or her counsel, taking the evidence on oath. The report, which exonerated Caroline on the main charge, nevertheless noted that her conduct "especially considering her exalted rank and station, necessarily give occasion to very unfavourable interpretations."[29] The vindication of the Princess Caroline did not end the matter. The whole subject was revived in 1813 after the Prince of Wales became Re-

---

brought the question of her status to the attention of Parliament. A secret committee of the House of Lords was established to consider the matter. The Marquis of Landsdowne then declared: "All secrecy was in its nature an evil, but occasions might occur in which it was necessary . . . . Secret committees had been appointed in cases of plots and conspiracies, and the proof of which depended on the evidence of persons whose names could not be revealed—in cases when the investigation related to individuals whom it was important to keep unapprized of the existence of any proceedings against them—in cases in which the interests of foreign states were concerned." *Parliamentary Debates,* New Series, "House of Lords," Vol. I, pp. 890–91 (June 7, 1820).

[28] By the Prince's request the Princess had been living apart from him since 1796, after the birth of the Princess Charlotte. It was alleged by Sir John and Lady Douglas that the Princess of Wales had given birth to a male child in 1802 and that the child was living with her. This accusation would, of course, had it been true, have had serious consequences for the succession to the Crown.

[29] The report was never officially printed. But with other documents it was prepared for the press by Spencer Perceval, who, however, withdrew it from circulation on taking office in 1807. It was reissued in 1813: *The Genuine Book. An Inquiry, or Delicate Investigation, into the Conduct of H.R.H. the Princess of Wales.*

gent, and the participants in the secret Commission expounded their parts before the House of Lords.[30]

The second "secret" Commission, known as the "Milan" Commission, was appointed in 1818 to gather evidence respecting the conduct of the Princess on the Continent, the intention being to decide upon a policy if the Princess should return to England and, perhaps (so far as Prince George was concerned), for the purpose of gathering information upon which to commence divorce proceedings. This report has never been published, but the evidence contained therein was undoubtedly the basis of the Attorney General's statement before the House of Lords in the trial of Queen Caroline (as she became after George III's death in 1820). The case[31] was ended by the Queen's death shortly after her failure to gain entrance to the coronation in Westminster Abbey.

SECURING EVIDENCE AND HOLDING HEARINGS

Despite the variety of uses to which the process of inquiry by Royal Commission has been put, it may be asserted that the very nature of the proceedings falls into a few fairly common and definite stages. First of all come preliminary meetings of the Commissioners at which there are questions to decide regarding the interpretation of the Reference, the holding of open or private meetings (or both), the nature and amount of evidence to be considered, the kind

[30] *Parliamentary Debates,* New Series, Vol. XXV, pp. 142 ff.

[31] The proceedings in the case during 1820–21 extend through the *Parliamentary Debates,* New Series, "House of Lords," Vols. I, II, and IV. The report of the "secret" committee of the Lords is to be found in Vol. II, pp. 167–68. The trial for adultery took the form of a Bill of Pains and Penalties (which is found at pp. 212–13) but finally came to nought.

and number of witnesses to be called, whether or not special investigators will be employed, and the general mode of procedure to be followed. Even the admittance of the public to meetings is considered a matter of the conduct of proceedings and therefore a question for the Commission, in each case, to decide.[32] The right to hold meetings and take testimony at places other than the seat of the government has always been admitted. The next stage, after the preliminary decisions have been made, is the process of getting at the evidence. This may be accomplished by the use of special investigators, by written evidence, or by oral interrogation of witnesses.

The first of these methods—and the use of special investigators—has been particularly commended as appropriate to social and political investigations. Those who are especially critical of the Royal Commission procedure or inquiry have recommended the extensive use of this type of research wherever it is applicable. In particular, the practice of delegating the work of local or special investigation to a staff of assistant Commissioners under the direction of a skilled expert has the approval of social scientists.[33] The assistant Commissioners chosen by the Royal Commission on Labour, appointed in 1891, received a definite and narrowly circumscribed reference and

[32] *House of Commons Debates,* 5th Series, Vol. 293, pp. 2130–31 (November 15, 1934).

[33] E.g., Sidney and Beatrice Webb endorse the results of the Commissions on the Poor Laws and on Municipal Corporations in 1834 and 1835 because of the reliance placed upon local investigations (*Methods of Social Study,* 1932, p. 148). Special investigators were used with noteworthy effect in the factory inquiry of 1833. Later the Trade Union Commission undertook special inquiries into the Sheffield and Manchester outrages in 1867, both of which reports were separately published (C. 3952 and 3980, 1867).

were prepared with full knowledge of the exact points upon which information was required. From the lucid reports[34] which the assistant Commissioners presented to the Royal Commission, a final report was drafted.[35] Occasionally, too, the Commissioners themselves engage in this type of investigation; but this may be regarded as a personal aberration of particularly enthusiastic members. It is commoner for the Commissioners to confine their personal activities to the study of evidence presented and to the public hearings. Yet these informal contacts on the part of the Commissioners are among the most valuable means by which the members conducting the inquiry can appreciate the human aspects of the subject they are investigating. The experience of ascertaining, even in a limited degree, the effect of laws and practices "on the spot" may be more revelatory of the state of affairs than any other more formalized procedure.[36]

[34] *Parliamentary Papers,* 1893–94: Vol. XXXV, C. 6894, pp. i–vi, C. 6894, p. xiii; Vol. XXXVI, C. 6894, p. xiv; Vol. XXXVII, C. 6894, p. xxv, C. 6894, p. xxiv, C. 6894, p. xxiii.

From these reports, the Webbs say, "We watch the investigator at work. He journeys from parish to parish; holds meetings of the labourers to elicit complaints; visits the workers' cottages; hobnobs with shepards, carters, and ploughmen in country lanes, rural markets, and auction marts; consults trade union and friendly society officials in informal chats; interviews ministers of religion of all denominations, poor law guardians and relieving officers, masters of workhouses, and inspectors of nuisances; takes counsel in the little towns with solicitors' auctioneers, estate agents, and everyone able to assist his inquiries; extracts, from the accounts of farmers, bailiffs, and landowners, actual statistics with regard to wages, perquisites, the prevalence of allotments, and the labor-bill per acre by large farms and small holdings respectively" (*Methods of Social Study,* pp. 148–49).

[35] *Parliamentary Papers,* Vol. XXXV, C. 7421, 1894.

[36] The information attained in these "miscellaneous" ways has been regarded by some, among whom are the Webbs, as "the most useful of all services rendered to sociology by these official inquiries" (S. and B. Webb, *op. cit.* p. 156).

The commonest method of gaining written evidence, i.e., as supplementary to special reports where investigators are employed, is the "questionnaire." The questionnaire, as used by Commissions, suffers from the defects which are common to all such rigid forms: The value of the results depends entirely upon the extent to which the questions actually attain the purpose of finding out the things which are really desired. Questions in printed form cannot bring to light new aspects of the subject; all they can do is provide a statistical elaboration of matters and opinions already in the mind of the questioner. Nevertheless considerable reliance is placed on this source of knowledge. It was even used by the Simon Commission of 1927, though in a form which permitted more elaborate replies than are usually desired. The questionnaire of this Commission was an invitation to submit memoranda. It was in outline form, and covered such main topics as: (*a*) the representative system as applied to British India; (*b*) the suitability of existing areas for governmental purposes; (*c*) the local self-governing bodies; (*d*) the problem of centralization; (*e*) the courts; and (*f*) the growth of education.[37] Among the other Royal Commissions which have used this method were those on Indian Currency and Finance, London Squares, Licensing, Land Drainage, Fire Brigades, and Police Powers and Procedure.[38]

[37] *Indian Statutory Commission,* "Extracts from Official Oral Evidence," Vol. XV, pp. 535–36.

[38] Cf. the *Reports* of these Commissions in *Parliamentary Papers,* on Indian Currency (1914), Vol. XIX, Cd. 7069, and Vol. XX, Cd. 7236; London Squares (1928–29), Vol. VIII, Cmd. 3196; Land Drainage (1927), Vol. X, Cmd. 2993; Fire Brigades (1923), Vol. XI, Cmd. 1945; Police Powers and Procedure (1928–1929), Vol. IX, Cmd. 3297.

Additional sources of valuable written information are to be found in the written reports presented by the department officials (which are nearly always of a high quality), in the reports from previous inquiries into various aspects of the subject, and in reports which have been prepared by experts for the Government on other occasions. There is, it is needless to say, a vast amount of statistical information in the current official reports and journals, since the publications of Government departments at the present time in nearly every country provide representative if not exhaustive surveys of almost every current social and political problem.

Public hearings have been utilized in nearly every inquiry of recent years. It is the practice for Commissions to invite all persons who are interested in the matter to present evidence which has any bearing upon the subjects included in the terms of reference. Then, from among those who express a willingness to testify orally before the Commission, a list of witnesses is drawn up by the chairman and the secretary, subject of course to approval by the Commission. It is here more than at any earlier stage that the influence of the chairman and the secretary begin to appear. The chairman, of course, will already have been prominent in arranging the order of business; and the secretary, throughout the inquiry, exercises his powers in providing for the clerical assistance (for copying documents, assembling and indexing reports, making available for the members the written materials, etc.).[39]

[39] It should be noted that in the postwar inquiries the secretary is rarely named in the warrant of appointment, as was the practice in

It is, then, at the open hearings, when oral testimony is taken, that the chairman's influence is first publicly felt. Indeed it may be said that the chairman occupies the key position in a Royal Commission. An American observer of British labor describes the work of Mr. Justice Sankey on the Coal Commission of 1919 as exemplifying the importance of a first-rate chairman: "He gives liberty to the witnesses to tell their story in their own way, and full scope to the commissioners for cross-examination." Possessing a brisk suavity, with a delightful smile, and a firm will, he never employed his rich humor against simple persons, ignorant and sincere. But when there was wrath at one witness, and the twelve Commissioners raised their voices together, the chairman rose and in his blandest tone said, "Thank you, gentlemen, thank you for all contributing at once." And when labor, in herd formation, trampled one famous expert "to the flatness of his own shadow," Sankey subdivided for them the limits of their "death-dealing function": "For questions of the industry, Mr. Smillie; statistical, Sir Leo [Chiozza Money]; policy, Mr. Webb." And he implied that treatment from one of them was enough for any particular authority who wandered into the witness

---

earlier years. The Newfoundland Commission of 1931 was an exception in this respect, owing no doubt to the peculiar authority (Canadian and Newfoundland as well as British) under which it was instituted. The secretary is usually a member of the highest rank of civil servants, deputed to the Commission either by the department concerned or by the Treasury. Proposals have been made for the formation of a permanent secretariat to undertake the work for all Commissions; but this suggestion did not meet with the approval of the Balfour committee and has never been adopted. The Balfour committee reported: "We consider the advantages of having one Permanent Secretary would be more than counterbalanced by the disadvantages, and we do not recommend this change" (*Balfour Report*, p. 14).

chair, which itself began to take on the "atmosphere of the electric chair."[40]

Such latitude of questioning may be productive under the capable leadership of a Mr. Justice Sankey. But, unfortunately, in the realm of oral evidence there are occasions when chairmen allow an inquiry to become pathetically unproductive by an unfortunate disinclination to curb irrelevant examinations and cross-examinations by well-meaning Commissioners. Students of a subject who have waited for the publication of the oral evidence of a Commission, with the hope that it will supplement their own inquiries or supply fresh material, have sometimes found that the output of new fact is negligible, and is buried, moreover, in a voluminous mass of absolute irrelevancies.

The hearings are the chief instrument of publicity at the command of the Commission, and the manner in which they are stage-managed may set both the tone for the proceedings and the public effect which will be produced by the report later. Frequently witnesses are expected to have presented written summaries of their testimony, upon which they will be orally examined. Indeed, it may be asserted that without this procedure the oral evidence will tend to be a chaos of unrelated and conflicting opinions and inconsequential speculations. The offhand fashion of extemporaneous questioning is not only expensive (stenographically, as well as in printing), but unless handled carefully is unproductive of constructive information or thought.[41] Complaint about the enor-

[40] Arthur Gleason, *What the Workers Want* (1920), pp. 33–34.

[41] "The slovenly habit, characteristic of distinguished personages on Royal Commissions and Government Committees of Inquiry unaware of

mous length of the "Minutes of Evidence," with its tens of thousands of questions covering a thousand or more pages has been expressed by hosts of critics.[42]

Skillful guidance during the hearings, or even advice outside the Commission rooms, by a tactful chairman, would save time and money and eliminate unimportant and useless pages of evidence. Of course, it is not beyond the competence of the distinguished personnel of many Commissions to spend less time in meaningless interrogation of witnesses, but most Commissioners (and many chairmen, too) are not, unless professionally trained, skilled in the difficult art of oral questioning. It is therefore the task of the chairman to conduct a Commission's work

---

the complicated network into which they are intruding, of extracting answers to vague and abstract questions such as, 'What in your opinion are the results of the legislative restriction on the hours of labour?' leads to a sleepy satisfaction arising not from fullness of knowledge but from mere intellectual flatulence" (S. and B. Webb, *Methods of Social Study* [1932], p. 71). At another place the Webbs, in a similar criticism of the Labour Commission of 1891, note that in the first five reports of this Commission the evidence was embodied in 96,333 questions and answers, mostly concerning abstract conundrums about all manner of social and legislative reforms. "The greatest triumph was, by skillful questions, to lead the witnesses, especially the working-men witnesses, into some logical inconsistency. One or other of us attended some meetings of the commission; and it was certainly entertaining to watch the dialecticians 'purring' at each other complacently when their little pounces came off," *ibid.*, pp. 143–44.

[42] Since 1927 (for reasons of economy) the practice of printing the volumes of evidence has declined very considerably; many Commissions now no longer publish verbatim reports of the public hearings, leaving the day-to-day reporting to the press. There is, however, no rule; sometimes the daily reports, as in the Arms Inquiry, are printed by the Stationery Office as nonparliamentary papers but are not reissued later. These "Minutes of Evidence" may appear several times (there may be one for each meeting, or one for every two or three meetings) before the final report appears as a "Command Paper." Undoubtedly it is a matter of discussion between the Commission and the Treasury in each case. Whether or not the pages are useless will probably always be a question, for it is clear that few people ever read these thick tomes after the report is issued.

as best he can and as quickly as possible along the most fruitful lines. He is particularly useful if he is capable of excluding irrelevant evidence and can cause the members to co-operate harmoniously in directing their inquiries straight to the heart of a question.

Except for this tendency to allow irrelevant questions—and the criticism does not hold for all—most chairmen of recent years have maintained a high standard of efficiency and public service. There have been, naturally, in the long line of Royal Commissions, some chairmen who were too conservative and therefore unlikely to allow any innovation in the technique of investigation. Some, in their effort to bring forth a unanimous report, have been too willing to allow compromises. Others, unfortunately, have been burdened (and dubious) by old age, weakness, laziness, or dullness. In no case can it be said definitely whether or not all pertinent witnesses are called or whether the appropriate ones have been chosen from those available. The Royal Commission on National Health Insurance, for example, admitted in its report[43] that it received very little evidence from insured persons, one of the most obvious sources of testimony. The main reliance for oral answers likely to lead to the solution of a problem is put upon a list of officials which usually includes: (1) permanent governmental officials who are in closest touch with the matter under consideration; (2) secretaries, officials, or other accredited representatives of the economic, political, or social groups vitally concerned;

[43] *Parliamentary Papers,* Vol. XIV, Cmd. 2596, 1926, p. 3.

(3) university professors or other specialists in the issue involved. Not always are all three categories included; but some Commissions, such as the one on Transport appointed in 1928, have an especially representative list of witnesses.[44]

When oral evidence from governmental officials is to be included it has been the usual practice, when it comes to important questions of policy, for responsible Ministers, rather than civil servants, however distinguished,[45] to present the views of their departments. As far as civil servants are concerned, there are no rules expressly governing their conduct when called as witnesses before Royal Commissions. Mr. Stanley Baldwin recently spoke in the House of Commons on this point, saying, in reference to civil servants called as witnesses: "A Royal Commission is entitled to receive from witnesses the benefit of their knowledge and experience, and the matter is therefore one to be governed not by rule but by practical considerations, the most important of which is that the Commission should receive every possible assistance in its investigations."[46]

In addition to the oral evidence from sources already mentioned, representatives of "lobby" organi-

[44] This Commission heard oral evidence from representatives of the following: Accident Offices Association; Associated Society of Locomotive Engineers and Firemen; Association of British Chambers of Commerce; Association of Municipal Corporations; Automobile Association; Board of Trade; Home Office; Ministry of Transport; Chief Constables' Association; Federation of British Industries; Lloyd's Underwriters; National Federation of Iron and Steel Manufacturers; Railway Companies Association; National Road Transport Employers' Federation; National Union of Railwaymen; Transport and General Workers' Union; and several other bodies. See *Parliamentary Papers*, Vol. XVII, Cmd. 3571, 1931, pp. 235–40.

[45] Cf. *House of Commons Debates*, 5th Series, Vol. 312, pp. 383–84.

[46] *Ibid.*, pp. 826–27 (May 18, 1936).

zations are sometimes asked to appear and give testimony before Royal Commissions. These organizations, many of which have headquarters near Parliament, are of the same character and purpose as in America; they approach members of the legislature, and send deputations to the departments (though they may not appear in Parliament, either on the floor or in committees). Some idea of the variety and range of these groups, as well as evidence of their appearance before Commissions, may be obtained by examining the lists of witnesses appended to the reports of certain Royal Commissions.[47]

As to the questions which are to be put to the witnesses: these are sometimes drawn up by the chairman (especially when he has been chosen because of skill in cross examination), and sometimes by the secretary. Any member of the Commission may ask questions, however, though this privilege is allowed to no outsiders.[48] When problems of unsolicited witnesses or of unsolicited evidence (written or oral) arise, each Commission must decide for itself what to do. Usually, after consideration by the chairman, the matter is brought to the attention of the other members for a decision as to the acceptability of the witness or of the evidence.[49] As to hearsay and sec-

[47] E.g., Royal Commission on Food Prices (*Parliamentary Papers*, Vol. XIII, Cmd. 2390, 1924–25); Royal Commission on Transport (*ibid.*, Vol. XVII, Cmd. 3751, 1931); Royal Commission on Licensing in England and Wales (*ibid.*, Vol. XI, Cmd. 3988, 1931–32); Royal Commission on Unemployment Insurance (*ibid.*, Vol. XIII, Cmd. 4185, 1932); Royal Commission on Coal Industry (*ibid.*, Vol. XIV, Cmd. 2600, 1926).

[48] J. T. Smith long ago severely criticized (*Government by Commissions Illegal and Pernicious*, p. 168) the practice of limiting oral questioning to members of the Commission only.

[49] See the recent discussion in the Commons concerning the volunteering of witnesses before the Commission on the Manufacture of and Trad-

ondary evidence, not founded on first-hand knowledge, the members are again their own judge of its acceptability. While this type of evidence has not been rigidly refused, some chairmen have attempted as far as possible, and with the help of the Commissioners generally, to exclude it. At the same time, other chairmen have held the view that it would not be wise to restrict the evidence before Royal Commissions in accordance with the practice in courts of law. Any difficulties as to the admissibility of questions proposed to be put by Commissioners have likewise been settled by each Commission for itself. Sometimes the majority have given in to the wish of the minority; and sometimes the minority, after discussion, have acquiesced in the decision of the majority. Usually, however, the chairman's decision has been accepted at the time though his ruling has been regarded as open for the Commission to discuss afterwards. Difficulties as to the rotation in which members put their questions have seldom arisen.

The advisability of introducing a more systematic procedure has been discussed from the very inception of the inquiry process. The Departmental Committee on the Procedure of Royal Commissions investigated the whole subject in 1910[50] but was unable to do more than suggest a draft circular for distribution among Commissioners as a guide to their inquiries. The difficulties which beset the organizer of procedure lie in the diversity of purposes, subjects,

---

ing in Arms. *House of Commons Debates*, 5th Series, Vol. 312, pp. 382–84 (May 13, 1936), and pp. 826–27 (May 18).

[50] It is interesting that, though it appeared from the report that numerous chairmen of commissions and others with experience were examined, no publication of the evidence occurred.

and composition of the Commissions. It is clear that not all inquiries can be conducted along the same lines. Some Commissions have a political basis as distinct from an expert or impartial foundation; others have as the topic for investigation a proposal which involves political discussion and compromise instead of the summing up of "exact" knowledge; and some consist of a score of Commissioners instead of but two or three members. Indeed, any attempt to stereotype or regiment the procedure would not only impair the value of the divergent types of inquisition but would impede the inquiries which profit by the present flexibility and formlessness of the "system," if such a term may be applied to it.

Nevertheless, it may be agreed that in so far as the purpose of an inquiry is to attempt the uncovering of elusive information and to make it possible for a specific group of men to weigh the ascertainable knowledge and to discriminate among divergent opinions, there are certain practices which can be utilized with greater productivity of result than others. A recent commentator has urged that "the way to authority is behaviour based upon a systematic recognition of certain principles of inquiry";[51] and a foreign student of administration has expressed an opinion derived from German experience that "the investigating process depends for its success on a regularized procedure which combines a reasonable measure of flexibility with consistency in the pursuit of clearly defined objectives."[52]

[51] H. F. Finer, *Theory and Practice of Modern Government*, II, 757.

[52] F. M. Marx, "Commissions of Inquiry in Germany," *American Political Science Review*, XXX (1936), 1134–43.

The difficulties which lie in the way of establishing a precise inquiry procedure spring, as has already been noted, from the transitory nature of the individual Royal Commissions, from their varying personnel, and from the many types of subject matter dealt with. In view of the non-institutionalized form of this mode of inquiry, the degree to which the most admirable features of the Commission procedure are realized depends upon the sagacity and experience of the Commissioners and in particular of the chairman. The expectation, therefore, that progress may come from more precise and definite modes of procedural practice is illusory. But this is not to say that certain methods of inquiry have not proved more efficacious than others.

It seems commonly agreed among those who have participated in inquiries, either as Commissioners or as witnesses, that the oral hearings are most valuable when they are used for the purpose of examining a witness upon previously written statements. Without previous statements in writing, the hearing is likely to become a cross examination with the purpose of entangling witnesses in a mass of dialectical contradictions. If this occurs, its usefulness for inquiry purposes ceases. At the same time it should be clear that any approach to "judicial" procedure is equally imperfect. So rarely does a Commission possess the power to command attendance of witnesses or to order the production of withheld papers that the proceedings must be regarded as essentially voluntary. Under these circumstances testimony must be freely tendered and, since there is no protection for the witness, much evidence can be procured only if the witnesses are assured of secrecy. Whether or not secret sessions should be held in order to encourage plain speaking by those who desire to remain anonymous is a matter for each Commission to decide. In general it may be said that (quite apart from considerations of liability for libel and slander) any evidence which witnesses do not desire to be connected with their names may be presented in a confidential written form. The most effective sources of information, as has been seen, are the reports of special investigators and the written evidence of recognized experts or persons thoroughly experienced in certain phases of the matter being investigated. The best results of the oral proceedings occur when the examination follows the study of these reports.[53] The opportunity is then provided for checking and analysis.

PRESENTING THE REPORT

When the Commission decides that sufficient evidence has been collected, it begins to draw up a report.[54] The time that elapses before such a decision varies, of course, according to the subject matter of

[53] Frequently the work of a Royal Commission has given rise to several books and numerous magazine articles; reports of commissions are often of such value as to warrant re-publication several years later. But it has rarely happened that the testimony of a witness is regarded so highly as to merit unofficial publication. There is, however, one interesting example: the answers to questions, memoranda, and oral evidence of Professor Alfred Marshall before the Royal Commission on Depression of Trade and Industry (1886), on Gold and Silver (1887), on the Aged Poor (1893), and on Imperial and Social Taxes (1897), together with his evidence before the Indian Currency Committee (1899) and his memorandum for the House of Commons on International Trade (1903), were reprinted after his death as *Official Papers by Alfred Marshall* (1926). They provide examples of evidence and memoranda at their best.

[54] Frequently specific parts of an inquiry are completed before the investigation, taken as a whole, may be closed. If so, "Interim Reports" —and there have been many of these—may be submitted before the final report appears.

the inquiry and the tendencies of the Commissioners: the duration of an inquiry is not set by law. The Commission on Honours (1922) lasted three months and submitted a report of fifteen pages; while the investigation begun in 1923 on Local Government continued for more than six years. The Commission on Agriculture, appointed in 1919, produced an "Interim Report" of twenty-one pages within a few months, but it never submitted a final report. The average life of Commissions since the World War has been about a year and a half.

Deliberation on the evidence, a summary of which has been prepared by the secretary, may take a long or a short time, depending on the degree of unanimity prevailing among the Commissioners. A rough draft report is usually prepared first; and this is ultimately shaped into a final report by the suggestions and alterations acceptable to the members. If unanimity of opinion proves impossible, there may be a "minority report" or even several minority reports. Also, individual Commissioners may agree "with reservations" to a report; or they may express individual opinions, either of a "concurring" or a "dissenting" nature, which are put into paragraphs appended to the report or which may be signed as separate memoranda. In addition to these possibilities, the majority may "reply" to the minority, their rebuttal being printed as part of the majority report. The Commission on Poor Laws which reported in 1909 made three kinds of recommendations: unanimous, majority (signed by fourteen members), and minority (signed by four members).[55] The Sankey

[55] *Parliamentary Papers,* Vol. XXXVII, Cd. 4499, 1909.

Coal Commission of 1919 had probably the most hopelessly divided membership in recent times. They submitted four separate final reports; and Mr. Justice Sankey, the chairman, supported one of the minority groups.[56]

As noted earlier, the Balfour Committee, which reported in 1910 on the procedure of Royal Commissions, urged in the strongest terms that every effort should be made to minimize differences among the members; and it went so far as to recommend that no Commission should have the clear right to present a minority report but that the presentation of such reports should be based upon a quorum vote of the Commission.[57] The basis for these recommendations was the belief that a unanimous report acquires greatly added weight and prestige, with an increased chance, therefore, of its recommendations being framed into legislation. And experience seems to indicate that two or more reports from various factions in a Commission does destroy the influence of an inquiry and tend to leave the ultimate decision entirely to political considerations.

The completed report is submitted by the chairman of the Royal Commission to the Home Office or to the department principally concerned. The report is then formally presented to the King, and "by command" it is laid before Parliament. It is unnecessary to recall here the long story of the development of the publication of such papers. By practice most reports of Royal Commissions are immediately

[56] *Ibid.*, 1919: Vol. XI, Cmd. 210; or Vol. XII, Cmd. 360.

[57] *Balfour Report*, paragraph 27, pp. 8, 12–14.

printed and are finally bound in the numerous annual volumes of *Parliamentary Papers,* occupying many pages of "Reports of Commissions."[58]

While much discussion has resulted from the irregularity of a Government withholding from Parliament a report which has been submitted to the King, there is no dispute as to the legality of such a course. In 1936 the exceptional period of three months elapsed between the completion of the Report of the Royal Commission on the Tithe-Rent Charge and its submission to Parliament by the Cabinet; but this was admittedly a breach of good practice.[59]

But with the submission of the final report the functions of the Royal Commission end; and His Majesty presents the chairman with a silver inkstand.

[58] The famous case of *Stockdale* v. *Hansard* (III *State Trials,* New Series, 723), involving the printer's liability for slanderous statements in a prison inspector's report, was the occasion for the passage of a statute in 1840 (3 & 4 Victoria, c. 9) staying proceedings resulting from the publication of papers printed by order of either House of Parliament upon the production of a certificate that such publication was by order of either House of Parliament. In the decision in *Houghton et al.* v. *Plimsoll* (1874, *Times,* April 2) it was held that the report of a Royal Commission presented to Parliament in printed form came within the scope of this protection.

[59] The Government's action as to the Tithe Report was regarded as something of a scandal and caused much discussion and questioning in the House of Commons. See *House of Commons Debates,* 5th Series, Vol. 307, pp. 259–60 (December 5, 1935); Vol. 307, pp. 546–47 (December 9, 1935); Vol. 307, p. 1422 (December 16, 1935); Vol. 308, pp. 45–46 (February 4, 1926); Vol. 308, pp. 557–58 (February 10, 1936); Vol. 308, p. 1116 (February 13, 1936); Vol. 308, pp. 1980–81 (February 19, 1936); Vol. 309, p. 23 (February 24, 1936). Such intervals were frequent early in the nineteenth century, as appears from *Parliamentary Papers,* XX, No. 301, 1827. And see p. 137, note 86.

CHAPTER VI

CONTEMPORARY DECLINE

There are some who are conciliated by Conciliation Boards. There are some who, when they hear of Royal Commissions, breathe again—or snore again.—G. K. Chesterton

NOTICEABLE DIMINUTION IN USE

Commencing with a fairly infrequent use at the beginning of the nineteenth century, Royal Commissions of Inquiry attained their widest extension in the middle of that century, at which time they had undergone a four- or fivefold growth. Thenceforth the number of such inquiries has gradually fallen until at the present time appointments have sunk again to the level of the first years of the nineteenth century. It must not be thought, however, that this development has proceeded at a uniform or regular pace. Taken year by year the number of new Commissions established appears most erratic; e.g., among the years with the most numerous creations are 1833 with 11, 1858 with 13, and 1868 and 1906 with 9 each. Yet even on a yearly basis the marked decline is noticeable. From 1831 to 1870 there were nineteen years in which the new Commissions numbered 6 or more; from 1870 to 1900 there were only three such years; and in the first third of the twentieth century only four such. Similarly it may be observed that prior to 1900 there were but three years in which only one Commission was appointed, though since that date this has been the case nine times. It is still true that we have not reached the point, frequently found in the early years of the nineteenth century, when there would be no Commissions appointed for a year or more; but every indication leads to the expectation that such a time is approaching.

Clear evidence of decline in the use of Royal Commissions is shown by viewing their creation over ten-year periods. It thus becomes evident that from the first decade of the nineteenth century, when fewer than 2 Commissions were appointed yearly (on the average), a progressive rise took place until 1851–60, when the annual average for the period was nearly 8. From that time on a noticeable fall may be perceived, a decline which, while checked temporarily in the last years of the nineteenth century and the early years of the twentieth, has proceeded quite definitely to the present day. At the commencement of this century it might have been thought that the decline in number was at an end and that some degree of stability (at about 4 new Commissions a year) had been obtained. The first ten years of the new century seemed to confirm this stabilization: between 1901 and 1910, 47 were appointed, an average of nearly 5 a year. The unexpected increase in the number of Commissions appointed by the new Liberal Ministry in 1906 (9), 1908 (7), and 1909 (6) even led the Balfour Committee on Royal Commissions[1] to assert as a "fact" in 1910 that "the number of Royal Commissions has been greatly increased in recent years." But this proved to be but a transient phase, often to be observed, though in a diminishing

[1] *Balfour Report,* p. 6.

degree, at the change of Ministry;[2] and the basic fall in new creations was soon renewed. From 1911 to 1920 there were 30 Commissions established; from 1921 to 1930, 28; and during the next five years (1931–35) only 10.[3] The decline in the use of Royal Commissions of Inquiry has thus been from an average of five a year to the low point of two. If the decline continues at this rate, in twenty years there will be no Royal Commissions at all. This development, however, is not very likely, though one may expect Commissions to become more and more rare in the course of the next few years.

At first sight it may be thought that the diminution in the number of Commissions in the recent period can be attributed to the existence of the National Government, on the ground that the indecisive and compromising nature of a coalition Ministry would explain the failure to utilize the inquiry procedure. There are two objections to this facile explanation. In the first place, the decline is in full accord with the prevailing long-run tendency of the last seventy years, a tendency which can be traced directly to other factors. Secondly, the National Government

[2] E.g., in 1929, when Labour came into power, the high mark for the postwar period was reached with five new Commissions.

[3] The following *Parliamentary Papers* are the sources from which the list of twentieth-century Commissions may be procured: 1904 (No. 315) LXXIX; 1913 (No. 159) LI; 1914–16 (Cd. 7855); 1916 (Cd. 8256); 1917–18 (Cd. 8741); 1917–18 (Cd. 8916). No list has been issued since 1917; for later Commissions the annual *Consolidated List of Stationery Office Publications* must be consulted. A useful classified index to Commissions since 1860 has recently been published in the United States: A. H. Cole, *A Finding-List of British Royal Commission Reports: 1860 to 1935* (Harvard University Press, 1935). The reason for this list commencing with 1860 is difficult to find, unless it be the unsatisfactory one that in 1862 the *Parliamentary Paper* (No. 317) contained a new heading, "Royal Commissions of Inquiry," instead of the older one, "Commissions of Inquiry."

TABLE IV

Royal Commissions in the Twentieth Century

Year	Number	Subjects
1901	4	Arsenical poisoning; Tuberculosis; Coal supplies; University education in Ireland
1902	5	Alien immigration; South African martial-law sentences; Civil service superannuation; South African war; Physical training in Scotland
1903	5	London transport; Volunteer forces; War-time food supplies; Trade disputes; St. Louis Exhibition
1904	5	Ecclesiastical discipline; Feeble-minded; Churches in Scotland; Old-age pensions in Australia; Navigation bill in Australia
1905	2	South African War Stores; Motor Cars Acts of 1896 and 1903
1906	9	Canals; Metropolitan police; Safety in mines; Coast erosion; Lighthouses; Vivisection; Shipping "rings"; Poor laws; Congestion in Ireland
1907	2	Church in Wales; Indian decentralization
1908	7	Whiskey; Land transfer; Ancient Welsh monuments; Ancient Scottish monuments; Ancient English monuments; Electoral systems; Allocations of Free and United Church property in Scotland
1909	6	London University education; Brussels, Rome, and Turin Exhibitions; Selection of justices of the peace; Divorce; Trade relations of Canada and West Indies; Mauritius
1910	2	Metalliferous mines (Health, etc); Public records
1911	2	Malta; Railway consolidation scheme of 1907
1912	5	Civil service; King's Bench delays; Natural resources of the Dominions; Indian public services; Scottish housing
1913	2	Indian finance and currency; Venereal diseases
1914	3	Landing of arms at Howth; Australia meat export; Sugar supply
1915	1	Defense of the Realm Losses
1916	7	Rebellion in Ireland; Arrest of Skeffington, etc.; Allegations against Jackson, Ltd.; Mesopotamia war; Dardanelles and Mesopotamia; Wheat supplies; University education in Wales

Year	Number	Subjects
1917	2	Paper supplies; Paper and wood pulp
1918	2	Proportional representation; Decimal coinage
1919	5	Agriculture; Coal industry; Awards to inventors; Income tax; Oxford and Cambridge Universities
1920	1	Dublin University
1921	4	Importation of store cattle; Compensation for damage by enemy action; Local government of Greater London; Fire brigades and fire prevention
1922	1	Honours
1923	3	Local government; Superior civil services in India; Mining subsidence
1924	4	Fine Arts; National health insurance; Lunacy and mental disorder; Food prices
1925	2	Indian currency; Coal industry
1926	3	Court of Sessions in Scotland; Indian agriculture; Cross-river traffic in London
1927	4	English and Welsh land drainage; National museums; London squares; Indian government
1928	1	Police powers
1929	5	Labor in India; Transport co-ordination; Licensing (England and Scotland); Civil service
1930	1	Unemployment insurance
1931	1	Malta
1932	1	Lotteries and betting
1933	2	Newfoundland; Durham University
1934	1	Business at common law
1935	5	Arms manufacture; Tithe; Safety in coal mines; Tyneside; Merthyr Tydfil
1936	1	Palestine

has not been backward in originating novel and quite fundamental departures from political, social, and economic practice; and in the course of so doing it has resorted to numerous other forms of inquiry.

To understand the full significance of the change that has been proceeding for a number of years it is necessary to investigate briefly certain other factors which have been operative in the recent past. It

NUMBER OF ROYAL COMMISSIONS, ANNUAL AVERAGE, BY DECADES, 1801–1936

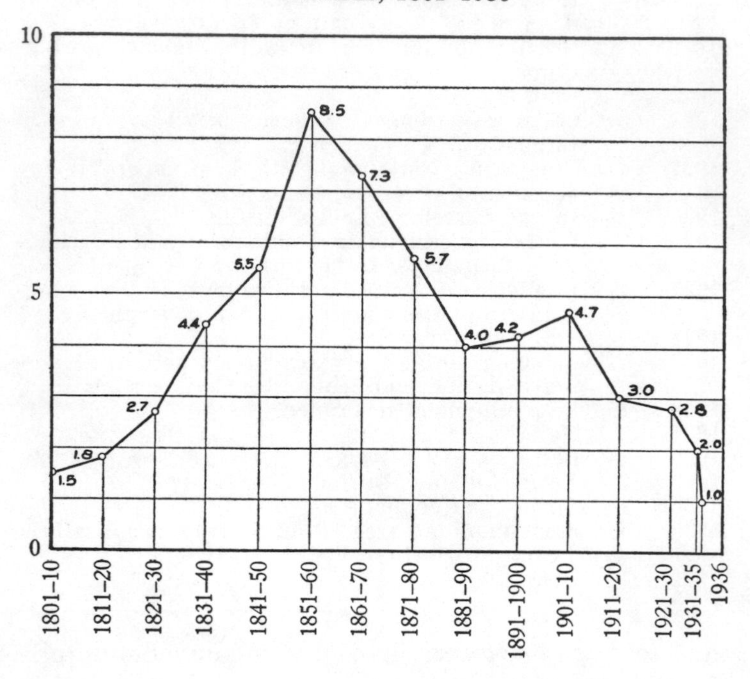

should be recalled that the very real reduction in the number of Royal Commissions of Inquiry is not an isolated process; it is, on the contrary, demonstrably related to the contemporary modes and institutions of English politics and government. This procedure was not adopted in the nineteenth century as the sole or unique means of political and social investigation, though it was the most successful method of that era. "Select Committees" of the two Houses of Parliament were simultaneously developed as complementary methods of inquiry. These select committees underwent a great expansion in use and number after the 1820's and then began to decline in the last two decades of the century. The average number reporting before 1830 stood close to 15; thirty years later this figure had doubled, and for a few years it was trebled. This rise occurred at the same time as the expansion in the use of Royal Commissions. But today, it is quite clear, the number of select committees has declined to the figure of a hundred years ago: In 1913 there were 21 committees; in the session of 1929–30 the number was 14. This last number seems about as low as the figure can conceivably fall. Of these 14 select committees, 9 were established to deal with purely parliamentary business — accounts and estimates, sittings of the House, procedure, etc. Two committees were devoted to local matters. And the remaining 3 were devoted to inquiry with a view to legislation or public policy. The objects of the latter inquiries—shop assistants, capital punishment, and musical copyright—were such as might quite properly be investigated either by committee or by Royal Commission. The reduction in the number of select committees has thus accompanied a similar contraction in the use of Royal Commissions.

The same factors tend to minimize the usefulness of both types of inquiry. Commissions and committees possess one noteworthy characteristic in common, the special *ad hoc* nature of their composition. Both are definitely established as unusual, if not extraordinary, agencies for the investigation of topics which are not otherwise readily dealt with by the ordinary political machinery. Each inquiry is an exceptional case; each investigating body is a transient and temporary organ specially created for a particular problem. It can be readily understood, therefore, that if the field of unprobed political subjects is reduced, the existing permanent organs of the government become more adequate for informational purposes, or a simpler method of research is discovered, the employment of these special agencies will greatly decline.

Such changes have in fact taken place. There are fewer unexplored questions; there is a more extensive organization of government departments; and there are new modes of conducting inquiry. This, of course, is not to say that the problems of the modern state have all been perceived and solved. It does not mean that the existing machinery of government is completely satisfactory and adequate for the complicated social and economic phases of modern society. Nor from this can it be inferred that a wisely planned administrative system has at last produced efficient advisory and research procedures. It does, however, seem to imply that new agencies and organs have appeared and are superseding the old and that fewer political problems are being left to the determination by unofficial (i.e., nonadministrative) and nonpartisan bodies. It may even be found that the new organs combine among themselves most of the advantages of Royal Commissions and select committees, together with some new benefits not heretofore found in these older agencies.

INFLUENCE OF ADMINISTRATIVE SERVICE

Superficially it may be thought that the most important change which has removed the necessity for inquiries such as are conducted by Royal Commissions is the growth of the administrative departments of Government. Clearly, there is a very noticeable parallel between the expansion of government services and the decline in the appointment of Commissions. If the rather considerable annual fluctuations are disregarded, it is apparent that the size of the civil establishments of the British departments remained fairly constant at an average of twenty to twenty-five thousand employees during the first forty years of the nineteenth century, the period in which Commissions were becoming more widely used. It was not until the commencement of the second half of the century that the number of civil servants was permanently doubled—in the 'seventies and 'eighties being somewhat over fifty thousand, at which point Royal Commissions were beginning to decline. After this the most rapid expansion in Civil Service took place; in the next twenty years the figure was again doubled, so that by the opening of the twentieth century the number of national employees was regularly over one hundred thousand. By the outbreak of the World War, the figure of 1901 had been multiplied more than two and a half times, and national employees numbered approximately two hundred and eighty thousand. Since the War, despite numerous reductions attempted in the name of economy, it has been found impossible to bring the number down to the prewar figure.

The importance of an extensive Civil Service does not come, however, from its size, except in so far as this indicates a close contact with society. The real importance of the ever widening administration is derived from the fact that it represents an increasing degree of social and economic control and regulation by government. The mere growth in numbers of civil servants, i.e., beyond the proportionate growth of the population, is not necessarily an indication of this, for it might proceed from the acquisition of a state monopoly such as the postal and telegraph services. But the growth of a diversified and expert senior personnel is of greater significance. Two consequences follow: The greater variety and multiplicity of contacts between administration and people, and the more intimate control and supervision exercised over hours of labor, health conditions, trade practices, and the like, has made increasingly available to government departments whatever information they desire on most points of social policy. In the second place, the enlargement of government services has been accompanied by a professionalization of the administration. After the reform of recruitment in 1855 and the establishment of a permanent board of selection (Civil Service Commissioners), the upper ranks of the government departments were not only removed from the earlier patronage and political influences but were more capable of increasing expert and specialized training. Thus, while the tentacles of state control were reaching into all phases of English social and economic life, a directing force of highly trained and intelligent civil servants was being organized and made capable of interpreting and reporting upon the conditions which their subordinates revealed. Not merely does each of the numerous government departments publish an increasing volume of statistical information, coupled often with analytical and explanatory pamphlets, but with such an experienced and qualified staff any administrative or parliamentary head may now obtain on fairly short notice adequate and satisfactory reports on almost every topic connected with the official business of the state.

It must not be imagined that Royal Commissions have been inactive or useless during this extension of administrative services. In addition to serving in the place of such organs before the latter were created, Royal Commissions have aided in two other ways. In the first place, it was the reports of the Commissions which provided the principles upon which many of the administrative developments should take place. This was true for the early "Reform" period inquiries as well as for the later ones. For example, the Hartington Report of the Royal Commission on military and naval departments, 1888, made proposals which may be regarded as anticipatory to the creation of the Committee of Imperial Defense. In the second place, as a direct re-

TABLE V

SEMI-PERMANENT ROYAL COMMISSIONS AFTER 1850

Duration and Subject of Commission	Dates
6 years	
New courts of justice (buildings) under the Courts of Justice Buildings Act, 1865	1865–71
River pollution	1868–74
Scientific instruction and the advancement of science	1869–75
Condition of the cathedral churches in England and Wales	1879–85
Electrical communication with lighthouses	1892–98
Vivisection	1906–12
Local government	1923–29
7 years	
Judicature	1867–74
Vaccination	1889–96
Sugar supply	1914–21
8 years	
Sewage of towns	1857–65
Educational Endowments (Scotland) Act, 1882	1882–90
9 years or more	
Public records (3d Report, 1919)	1910–19
Wheat supplies	1916–25
Patriotic fund (Dissolved in 1904 by Act of Parliament)	1854
Horse breeding (Final Report, 1911)	1887
Crofter colonization (15th Report, 1906)	1888
Sewage disposal (Final Report, 1915)	1898
Tuberculosis (Final Report, 1911; final appendix, 1915)	1901
Awards to inventors (6th Report, 1931)	1919

sult of the reports of Royal Commissions of Inquiry permanent bodies have been established. Often the Commissions have continued their inquiries over many years;[4] and frequently some of these permanent bodies have been little more than former Royal Commissions now provided with a statutory basis for their investigative and administrative duties. There are numerous examples of Commissions which have become completely institutionalized.[5]

INCREASE IN USE OF COMMITTEES AND BOARDS

It is natural that with the growth of administrative oversight and the extensive knowledge of social conditions which is placed at the disposal of the political ministerial heads there should be less need of the appointment of Royal Commissions simply for the purpose of procuring "information." This is unquestionably the case. The more technical the subject of inquiry or the more specialized the type of material to be investigated, the more it is found that the Government officials and the independent professional "experts" alone are capable of conducting

[4] See Table V.

[5] The following are the chief permanent commissions today: (*a*) Civil Service; (*b*) Crown Lands; (*c*) Forestry; (*d*) Charity; (*e*) Railway and Canal; (*f*) Exhibition of 1851; (*g*) Historical Manuscripts; (*h*) Welsh Church Temporalities; (*i*) Church Estates; (*j*) Ancient and Historical Monuments and Constructions (one each for England, Scotland, Wales, and Monmouthshire); (*k*) English and Scottish Special Areas; (*l*) Newfoundland Commission of Government; and (*m*) Fine Arts. The original Royal Commission on Fine Arts, appointed in 1841, issued its thirteenth report in 1863. A new Fine Arts Commission was appointed in 1924 and by 1931 had issued four reports. According to the terms of reference of the latter Fine Arts Commission, the members were to continue as a working body but from time to time were to be given new duties by one or the other of the Departments (see *Parliamentary Papers*, Vol. IX, Cmd. 2228, 1924, pp. 2–3). In 1933 the Government decided that in the future, on questions involving aesthetic and other similar considerations, such as town planning, independent advisory opinions should be obtained and a small committee would be appointed by the Prime Minister to advise the Minister on such questions when they arose. The Royal Fine Arts Commission, at the same time, would still be consulted on occasion as before (see *Annual Register*, 1933, p. 8).

effectively and with speed the requisite investigation. Only in so far as it is desirable to provide both non-expert and common-sense public representation does the Royal Commission of Inquiry on such matters as public health, social insurance, education, or money and banking have any purpose. In the various departments there are comprehensive reports by inspectors of factories, schools, mines, prisons, and local constabulary; by medical officers on children's health, workers' conditions, and the special inquiries into explosions, wrecks, railway accidents, road casualties, etc. In addition to this the several departments prepare voluminous reports of statistics on such topics as trade and commerce, industrial and agricultural production, crime and punishment, and housing and education.

The reports of individual Ministers, their deputies, and their specially appointed agents should also be mentioned. One official to be noted in this connection is the Government Actuary; another is the Parliamentary Counsel. More similar to investigations conducted by Royal Commissioners, however, was a single-handed inquiry into conditions in Palestine undertaken in 1930 by Sir John Hope Simpson. Instructed by the Secretary of State for the Colonies, this gentleman completed a local inquiry in Palestine and also visited Trans-Jordan to consider relevant matters there.[6] There are dozens of such reports resulting from special inquiries by official and nonoffi-

[6] The Simpson Report, embodying definite conclusions and recommendations for British policy in regard to land settlement, immigration, and general development of Palestine, was issued in October of 1930 (*Parliamentary Papers*, Vol. XVI, Cmd. 3686, 1930–31, "Palestine Report on Immigration, Land Settlement, and Development"). For conclusions and recommendations, see especially pp. 74–91, 141–53.

cial investigators,[7] for, in the many phases of social life upon which further information is required, the executive departments of the Government have provided themselves numerous new substitutes for the formal Royal Commission type of inquiry.

Two things are clearly revealed by a study of the many procedures which are employed within the administrative system. The first is that in addition to the ordinary reporting and inquiring functions of the regularly organized civil establishment there are an unbelievable number of subsidiary and supplementary committees at work. Between sixty and seventy different committees, boards, or councils presented published reports in 1935.[8] The greatest extension of their use took place, as one might expect, during the course of the World War. By 1916, 94 committees and boards had been set up for War purposes; at the close of 1917 the number of bodies established to consider "Public Questions Arising out of the War" had increased to 267, of which only 7 were Royal

[7] An amusing example of embarrassment caused by a Cabinet change in the midst of such an inquiry may be found in the McDougall Report of 1929 respecting imperial trade. Several studies of this subject had been set on foot by the Conservative Government prior to 1929. When the second Labour Government came into office in that year, some of the Ministers found themselves presented with reports which they regarded as both misleading and contrary to sound imperial policy. The new Labour Secretary of State for the Dominions (Lord Passfield) wrote the foreword to the McDougall Report although he found himself forced to deplore its thesis and deny its validity. *Vide* F. L. McDougall, *The Growing Dependence of British Industry upon Empire Markets* (H.M. Stationery Office, 1929), Preface.

[8] It is beyond the scope of this monograph to make a complete study of this development. A count of the committees whose reports are scattered through the 238 pages of the *Consolidated List of Government Publications* for 1935 gave approximately seventy such reporting committees. A reading of the reports from the Committees of Public Accounts and from the Select Committees on Estimates during the past five years demonstrates the further fact that these types of research and inquiry are both recognized and supported by parliamentary authority.

Commissions. Alongside these there were 87 other committees, etc., appointed to investigate public questions "which will arise at the close of the War,"[9] only 2 of them being Royal Commissions. Thus, for every Royal Commission created for inquiry purposes in the World War, there were some fifty advisory and investigating bodies of other types. The great extension of administrative committees could not remain long at such a level, and there was a pronounced decline after 1920. Nevertheless these methods of inquiry—single investigators, department committees and advisory boards, interdepartmental committees, and the like—have continued to be at least ten times as numerous as the Royal Commissions of Inquiry in the postwar years.

The second and perhaps the most remarkable feature of this new development is the extreme flexibility and adaptability of the procedure. The new bodies which are used for inquiry purposes vary from the stabilized statutory organs established by parliamentary authority for the purpose of advising a Minister, or of watching the operation of a statute, all the way to *ad hoc* ephemeral bodies informally set up by one or two administrative heads to inquire into internal department matters or to consult with allied administrative organs on common problems.

Precision of statement respecting these innumerable bodies is impossible because they are completely unorganized and are indiscriminately distributed throughout the Government services. Confusion is

[9] The lists of World War inquiries are to be found in the following *Parliamentary Papers:* Cd. 7855, 1914–16; Cd. 8256, 1916; Cd. 8741 and Cd. 8916, 1917–18.

worse confounded as there is consistency of neither nomenclature nor composition. In general, however, it may be said that they fall into three large classes: departmental or interdepartmental committees; advisory councils; and department or interdepartment committees.

The first of these, the departmental or interdepartmental committees, are generally so named in their titles. In reality they are Royal Commissions of Inquiry in all but formal appointment. Their members are prominent politicians, economists, business men, or publicists who are appointed for the consideration of a problem in all respects identical with those formerly, and still, studied by Royal Commissions. The only difference between a departmental committee and a Royal Commission, for all practical purposes, is that the former lacks the aura of dignity and eminence to be derived from the title of "Royal Commission" and the possession of a royal warrant of appointment.[10] Generally speaking, the departmental committees are appointed by a Treasury "minute"—this is practically always the case for interdepartmental committees — though when their establishment is due to the initiative of a particular Minister they are set up by authority of the department concerned. The reports of several of these committees have been, in recent years, far more important than the reports of many Royal Commissions.[11]

[10] "A departmental committee is appointed by the political head of a government department, and consists of such persons, officials and others, as he may select. Its functions and powers are much the same as those of a royal commission, but it is supposed to be a rather less dignified body" (Sir Courtney Ilbert, *The Mechanics of Law Making* [1914], p. 71).

[11] Among the most noteworthy have been the Committees of Recon-

The second type of new committee is the permanent advisory body. These may be compared to the Royal Commissions which in the course of time became permanent agencies either by statute or by continued reappointment. These new bodies are generally set up in a purely advisory capacity, though with permanent existence within a department. Almost every administrative department now has one or more such advisory organs, each usually known as "general advisory council," though in certain departments they are given other designations, e.g., Advisory Committee on Education (Colonial Office), Statutory Committee (Ministry of Labour), Departmental Committee (Ministry of Health). There are, besides these examples, about half a dozen other committees with different titles.[12] It will be evident that, like the departmental committees, these bodies are so flexible that they can be made official and expert, representative and political, or technical and impartial agencies for research.

Finally, there are the innumerable and more obscure transient committees established for temporary purposes within the departments or extending across the boundaries of departmental organization. They can be called department committees or interdepartment committees for lack of any other name. In

---

struction during and after the War; the "Balfour Committee" on Industry and Trade (Cmd. 3282, 1929); the "May Committee" on National Expenditure (Cmd. 3920, 1931); and the "Macmillan Committee" on Finance and Industry (Cmd. 3897, 1931).

[12] E.g., the Mines Department has a Safety in Mines Research Board in addition to two other "committees"; and the Scottish Office has almost all of the varieties possible: a Herring Industry Board, Educational Endowments Commissions, four "Advisory Committees" and a Standing Committee on the National Library.

most cases they will be composed of officials of the departments concerned—and this is one of the easiest ways to differentiate them from departmental committees. Needless to say, many of their findings are never made public, since their purpose may be to elucidate some point upon which the executive heads desire information for administrative purposes. Yet their reports are often published and at times form the basis for legislative action. Sometimes nonofficial members are invited to participate; and the committee, which may have arisen as a special internal inquiry, takes on the form and function of a departmental committee with public implications.

One feature to be noted in regard to these new procedures of inquiry is the ease with which they may be altered or enlarged in order to enable the state to penetrate every phase of social activity, voluntary, individual, or public. An example of fluidity and adaptability of procedure to meet special cases as they arise is given in the pages of one of the publications of the Board of Education, "The Health of the School Child." This document, it may be mentioned, is to be found in the *Annual Report of the Chief Medical Officer of the Board of Education,* for 1934. "In the autumn of 1934 the Milk Marketing Board for England and Wales appointed a committee . . . . to advise and assist that Board in regard to the expenditure of the funds made available by section II of the Milk Act of 1934 for the purpose of increasing the consumption of milk. This Committee . . . . after an informal conference, attended by representatives of the Board, various Governmental Departments, the Medical Research Council and the

Advisory Committee, decided that an investigation should be undertaken with the object of comparing the nutritive value of milk for the growth and development of school children, and that those in attendance should constitute a supervising committee. This body is called the Milk Nutrition Committee.

"The latter Committee agreed to place the conduct of the scientific side of the research in the hands of a sub-committee composed of representatives of the Ministry of Health, the Ministry of Agriculture and Fisheries, the Board of Education, the Department of Agriculture for Scotland, the Department of Health for Scotland, the Scottish Education Department, the Medical Research Council, and the Rowett Research Institute, in conjunction with the representatives of the National Union of Teachers and Officers of the Milk Marketing Board for England and Wales, and the Scottish Milk Marketing Board."[13] The informality and flexibility of consultation and research permitted by such collaboration is quite clearly one of the reasons why Royal Commissions have been superseded by these newer agencies.

EFFECTS OF PARTY PROGRAMS AND CONFERENCES

Thus far the decline of Royal Commissions of Inquiry has been attributed to the growth of an elaborate administrative system which has provided new modes of investigation into the social and economic conditions of the country. Commissions are less necessary today because an expert civil service keeps

[13] *Annual Report* (as cited in the text), p. 31. Upon this whole question of interdepartmental relations, *vide* the informative chapter in W. I. Jennings, *Cabinet Government*, 1936, chapter vi.

the administrative and parliamentary heads more or less completely informed of the working of the existing laws and of the need for their alteration as the social structure changes. Moreover, to supplement the regular and routine procedures for securing information the executive departments have commenced to utilize a number of research and inquiry methods—special investigators, department committees, etc.—which obviate the need for the occasional Commission inquiry. A dozen or more of these new bodies have been given parliamentary approval by statute or by financial support. Further, the flexibility of this novel machinery permits its use as an aid in bringing greater efficiency and harmony into the activities of the administrative services where they have overlapping or common functions or where they need new organs to introduce a greater compatibility with industrial, commercial, or social groups. And, lastly, it is clear that the nonofficial departmental or interdepartmental committees of the present type are able to perform the same tasks as the older Commissions and to employ the same type of personnel. The newer bodies, then, possess all the advantages (except that of dignity) of the Royal Commissions, together with certain additional benefits.

There still remains to be discussed the political aspect of the decline of Royal Commissions. The latter, it will be recalled, gained their significance not only because they investigated many of the unprobed problems of nineteenth-century industrialism upon which information was lacking but also because they presented the Government of the day with authoritative ready-made solutions of questions with which the Cabinet was either incapable of dealing or for which it feared to take responsibility unaided. Commissions thus had an important use in so far as they offered acceptable policies endorsed by experienced and reputable representatives or impartial Commissioners. This policy-suggesting function of Commissions of Inquiry has now been undermined by two modern developments.

The first of these developments proceeds directly from the increasing regimentation of political parties. Whatever may be the constitutional consequences of recent party organization,[14] there can be no doubt that there has been a marked tendency for parties to bind electors and politicians together by means of precise and definite political programs. It may be true that the Reform Whigs of a century ago had fairly specific ends in view when they appealed to the limited electorate of their day; but the Reform elections were an exception to the general practice. After the fury of reform had spent itself, and after the purposes had been obtained, the opposing parties did not face each other with definite platforms to which the leaders had been pledged. Elections might be won upon specific issues; but, in general, throughout the greater part of the nineteenth century, statesmen were restrained, as all the Ministers now are, by the detailed provisions of a comprehensive program. As the century drew to a close, however, the creation of national electoral organizations, i.e., bodies appealing to the voters with systematized doc-

[14] J. R. Muir, *How Britain Is Governed* (1930), chapter iv.

trines and slogans, ushered in the change which has gradually reduced the parliamentary members to the position of disciplined and subordinated partisans of a political program. The Conservative party has been least submissive to doctrinal elaboration; but even this organization has witnessed increasing definiteness of policy in the leader's manifesto or letter to the nation. The Liberal and Labour parties, on the other hand, have vied with each other in offering to the voter comprehensive programs for acceptance or rejection. Not content with the general or specific resolutions by party conferences, the Liberal and Labour leaders have presented to the electorate extensive doctrinal programs, with elaborate proposals on all conceivable matters, embodied in books and pamphlets.[15]

Without entering into the controversy over "Men versus Principles," and without inquiring whether, in fact, the party leaders have adhered to the programs which they put forward for election purposes, it must be clear that the tendency of such party programs must be to reduce the freedom of the successive Cabinets so far as acceptance of policies recommended by Royal Commissions of Inquiry is concerned. The example of 1931, when the Labour Government found itself unable to accept the economies proposed by "impartial" investigations, may be an exceptional case; but it does illustrate the possible consequences of party pledges upon free action by the Government.

The increasingly specific nature of the programs

[15] E.g., *The Liberal Way* (1934); *Labour and the Nation* (1928); etc.

of modern political organizations has restricted the field within which Ministries may follow the recommendations of impartial inquiring bodies on public questions of a controversial type. There is a second development which has served to remove disputed subjects from the purview of Royal Commissions. This is the invention of a substitute organ to take the place of representative Commissions. One of the chief objections to the Royal Commission of Inquiry which did, in fact, represent the partisan or interested groups was the pretense of impartiality. As purely investigative bodies, these representative Commissions were unsatisfactory devices; as agencies for the partisan discussion of political issues, they were a sham. It is true that with the several interested groups or political parties accorded equal representation a Royal Commission might be occasionally successful in finding an acceptable compromise on a controverted topic, but this success did not flow from the nature of the body as a Commission of Inquiry. The benefits derived from such representative Commissions as attained useful agreement in serious disputes sprang from the Commission being in reality a conference of the parties interested in the question. It is the perception of this fact which has encouraged increasing reliance upon conferences for the attainment of practicable and acceptable solutions on disputed public topics in recent years. A "conference" differs, however, from a "representative" Commission primarily in the openly recognized "interested" complexion of its membership. The members are admittedly delegates or representatives designated by the industrial, social, or political groups concerned in the problem. Instead of being Royal Commissioners professing a false impartiality, members of a conference are definitely spokesmen for their respective organizations or sponsors.

So important has the conference method become that it may be asserted that this is now the characteristic process to which the Government turns when it has not cared to take full responsibility, when the matter has not been settled by decision of the electors, or when the usual political channels have failed to produce a solution. The outstanding examples of resort to this procedure are: Irish Home Rule (1914); electoral procedure (1916–17); Irish Constitution (1917); House of Lords reform (1917–18); industry (1919); imperial policy (especially 1926 and 1932); and Indian government (1931–33). The fact that most of these conferences were unsuccessful in attaining the desired agreement on policy should not blind us to the extent to which the procedure is used on major issues. Numerous failures may lead to the disappearance of the conference method unless some new devices are introduced to eliminate the very same defects which have nullified the efforts of representative Royal Commissions.[16] The point to be noted here, however, is that while party programs are tending to narrow the field within which political compromise and agreement can be attained, a new form of partisan investigation and discussion has been introduced to supersede the Royal Commission.

[16] It may be pointed out here that no satisfactory method of distributing representation (other than by population) has yet been invented. All types of economic council, industrial board, labor court, etc., have been forced to fall back on equal representation with or without disinterested chairmen when they did not use some form of population basis.

CONCLUSION

What then remains of Royal Commissions of Inquiry? If the research function has been assumed by new administrative devices, and if the policy-aiding function has been diminished by new political developments, is there any task left for Commissions to perform? Two answers can be given.

In the first place, though inquiry and consideration may be progressively passing into the hands of other bodies, it is not yet true that the latter have completely superseded the Royal Commission. Other organs may perform these duties; but other organs are not always used. Royal Commissions may be displaced to a considerable degree, but they are not discredited. An expert inquiry may be undertaken with greater knowledge and insight by official or technical committeemen, and a political discussion may be undertaken more acceptably and fruitfully by a "conference" or round table of politicians and delegates than by a nonexpert or nonrepresentative Commission. Yet the most admirable and characteristic feature of the best Royal Commissions—the special combination of knowledge and wisdom on the part of the members and of investigation and discussion in procedure—has not been duplicated in any of the new agencies, unless it be in the departmental and interdepartmental committees which are Commissions in all but royal appointment. Successive Governments will undoubtedly find it advisable to make use of Royal Commissions (or the less imposing departmental committees) whenever they are faced with difficult subjects requiring this union of authoritative information and experience.

In the second place, there remains what is perhaps the most significant aspect of the modern Royal Commission—its usefulness in publicizing in a non-partisan manner a topic on which the public is ill-informed. The aura of royal approval, which appointment by the Crown accords to inquiry by Royal Commission, provides an admirable setting for the educative task of such investigations. Through the devices of public hearing and through the publicity attendant upon the presentation of the report, attention is focused upon the issue in hand, support for a reasonable solution is mobilized, and sinister, selfish, and antagonistic interests are driven under ground or neutralized. It may be true that Royal Commissions are often resorted to by a Government under pressure of public opinion with the hope of shirking responsibility or of postponing action. But it is evident that this can never be the chief use, for the appointment of a Commission would soon be recognized as an evasion rather than an attempt at solution.

Every indication today points to the conclusion that the Golden Age of Royal Commissions is over. This ancient procedure is, however, still so deeply entrenched by virtue of its antiquity, past utility, and present prestige that it may not be suffered to disappear. Royal Commissions of Inquiry may continue to serve as occasional and still influential agencies where eminent persons are required for the study of important questions and where the luster of royal appointment is helpful in creating a favorable political reception for their recommendations.

APPENDIX

In the pages which follow are provided documents of importance—and one merely of interest—in connection with the evolution of British Royal Commissions of Inquiry.

A. DOMESDAY BOOK

WRIT FOR AN INQUEST OF LANDS AT ELY

[1080. Translation by Adams, George Burton, and Stephens, H. Morse, *Select Documents of English Constitutional History* (New York, 1919), p. 2]

William king of the English, to Archbishop Lanfranc, and to Roger Count of Mortain, and to Godfrey Bishop of Coutances, greeting.

I order and direct you to assemble again all the shires which were present at the trial held concerning the lands of the church of Ely, before my consort went to Normandy the last time. With them, also, let there be those of my barons who had the right to be present at the aforesaid trial and who hold lands of the same church. When they have come together, let there be chosen some of those Englishmen who know how Edward died, and what they say about it let them, thereupon, witness by an oath. This done, let there be restored to the church the lands which were in its demesne on the day of the death of Edward, excepting those which men claim that I have given to them. With regard to these, signify to me by letters which they are and who hold them. But let those who hold lands by service, which, without doubt, ought to be held from the church, make the best agreement they can with the abbot, and if they refuse, let the lands remain to the church. Let this also be done concerning those who hold sac and soc. Finally, order those men who hitherto by my order and direction have been accustomed to do it, to keep in repair the bridge at Ely.

B. INQUEST OF THE SHERIFFS

[1170. Translation by Adams and Stephens, *op. cit.*, pp. 18–20]

In the first place, the barons shall require bond and surety from all the sheriffs who have been sheriffs since the lord king last went over to Normandy, and from all who since that time have been bailiffs or ministers of theirs who have held a bailiwick from them and from all those who since that time have held the hundreds of the barons which they have in the county whether they hold them at a term or in custody; that on a day which they shall set for them they will appear before the lord king to do justice and to redress to him and to his men what they ought to redress. And if because of sickness the sheriffs shall be unable to appear before them, let them send in their place persons to answer for them, and let these give bond and surety sufficient for the sheriffs and for themselves, that they will perform in the presence of the lord king that which the sheriffs ought to perform on the fixed day.

Afterwards they shall take an oath from all the barons and knights and freemen of the county, that they will speak the truth concerning that which shall be inquired of them on behalf of the lord king, and that they will not conceal the truth for love of any one, or for hatred, or for bribe or reward, or for fear or premise or for any reason.

This shall be the manner of the inquest:

I. In the first place let inquisition be made concerning the sheriffs and their bailiffs what and how much they have received from each hundred, and from each vill and from each man, since the lord king went abroad, whence the land and the people have been burdened; and what they have received by a judgment of the county or hundred, and what without a judgment, and what they learn was taken by a judgment, let it be written down by itself, and what without a judgment let it be written down by itself; and concerning all exactions inquisition shall be made of the cause and the evidence.

II. Likewise let inquisition be made concerning the archbishops, bishops, earls and barons, and their stewards and officers, what and how much they have received from their lands, since the said term, from each of their hundreds, and from each of their vills, and from each of their men, by a judgment or without a judgment, and let them write down separately all these exactions and their causes and occasions.

III. And likewise let inquisition be made concerning those men who since that term have held in custody other bailiwicks from the lord king, whether of a bishopric, or of an abbey, or of a barony, or of any honor or escheat.

IV. And likewise let inquisition be made concerning the king's bailiffs who have travelled through his land to do the king's business, which has been assigned to them; and what they learn from this, let them write down.

V. Also concerning the chattels of those who fled because of the Assize of Clarendon and concerning the chattels of those who have been undone through that assize, let inquisition be made of what has been done and of what was obtained thence in each hundred and each vill, and let it be diligently and carefully written down. And likewise let inquisition be made whether any one has been unjustly accused under that assize for reward or promise or hatred or other unjust cause; and whether any accusation has been withdrawn or any accused person released for reward or promise or love and who received the reward for it, and likewise let this be written down.

VI. And let inquisition be made concerning the aids for marrying the king's daughter, what was obtained thence in each hundred and each vill, whether in payments or in remissions, as to whom this has been handed over and paid.

VII. And let inquisition be made of what and how much the foresters and their bailiffs and officers have received, since the said term, in their offices in whatever way they received it or under whatever circumstance, and whether they have remitted any of the rights of the king for reward or promise or for any friendship. And concerning forest offenses; concerning those who have injured his forests and stags and other wild beasts; and what they learn, let them write down diligently; and whether the foresters or their bailiffs have arrested any one or attached any one by bond and surety or have accused any, and afterwards have released them without trial on their own responsibility, and let inquisition be made concerning those who have done these things and let it be written down.

VIII. And let all who have been accused of anything be placed under bond and surety to appear before the lord king at a time which shall be appointed for them, and to do right and to redress to the king and to his men what they ought to redress, and let those without sureties be held in custody.

IX. And inquisition shall be made whether the sheriffs or any bailiffs have returned any of the things which they have taken or whether they have made any peace with men since they heard of the arrival of the lord king, to prevent any complaint from thence reaching the lord king.

X. And let inquisition be made concerning amercements whether any one has been released, for reward or love, from what he had at first been amerced, and by whom this has been done.

XI. And let inquisition be made concerning those who owe homage to the lord king and have done it neither to him nor to his son, and let them be written down.

XII. Concerning the demesnes of the lord king, let inquisition be made whether the houses are enclosed with ditch and hedge, and whether there are granaries there, and cow-sheds, and sheepfolds and other buildings and stock, as the lord king ordered before he went abroad.

XIII. And after they have been examined, my sheriffs and officers shall employ themselves about my other affairs, and they shall swear to attend lawfully to making the inquest throughout the lands of the barons.

C. ENCLOSURES

[1517. From A. E. Bland, P. A. Brown, and R. H. Tawney, *English Economic History-Select Documents* (London, 1915), pp. 262–64]

The King to his beloved and faithful John Veysy, dean of our Chapel, Andrew Wyndesore, knight, and Roger Wegeston, late of Leicester, greeting. Whereas of late in times past divers our lieges, not having before their eyes either God or the benefit and advantage of our realm or the defence of the same, have enclosed with hedges and dykes and other enclosures certain towns, hamlets and other places within this our realm of England, where many of our subjects dwelt and there yearly and assiduously occupied and exercised tillage and husbandry, and have expelled and ejected the same our subjects dwelling therein from their holdings and farms, and have reduced the country round the houses, towns and hamlets aforesaid, and the fields and lands within the same, to pasture and for flocks of sheep and other animals to graze there for the sake of their private gain and profit, and have imparked certain great fields and pasture and woods of the same in large and broad parks, and certain others in augmentation of parks for deer only to graze there, whereby the same towns, hamlets and places are not only brought to desolation, but also the houses and buildings of the same are brought to so great ruin, that no vestige of the same at the present is left, and our subjects, who have dwelt in the said places and there occupied and exercised tillage and husbandry, are now brought to idleness, which is the step-mother of virtues, and daily live in idleness, and the crops and breeding of cattle that were bred and nourished by the same tillers and husbandmen dwelling in the same towns, hamlets and places for human sustenance, are withdrawn and entirely voided from the same places, and the churches and chapels there hallowed are destroyed and divine services there taken away, and the memory of souls of Christians buried there utterly and wholly perished, and many other inestimable damages grown therefrom and daily hereafter will grow, to the greatest desolation and undoing of our realm and diminution of our subjects, unless an opportune remedy for the reformation of the same be swiftly and speedily applied: We, as we are duly bound, desiring to reform the aforesaid and wishing to be certified touching the same, what and how many houses and buildings have been thrown down from the feast of St. Michael the Archangel in the fourth year of the reign of the most illustrious lord Henry, late King of England, the Seventh, our father, and how many and how great lands which were then in tillage are now enclosed and converted to pasture, and how many and how great parks have been imparked for the feeding of deer since the same feast, and what lands have been enclosed in any parks or any park, which then were or was, for the amplifying and enlarging of such parks, have therefore appointed you and two of you to enquire by oath of good and lawful men of the counties of Oxford, Berks, Warwick, Leicester, Bedford, Buckingham, and Northampton, as well within liberties as without, and by other ways, manners and means whereby you shall or may the better learn the truth, what and how many towns, how many houses and buildings have been thrown down from the aforesaid feast, and how many and how great lands which were then in tillage are now converted to pasture, and how many and how great parks have been enclosed for the feeding of deer on this side of the same feast, and what lands have been enclosed in any parks or any park, which then were or was, for the enlargement of such parks, and by whom, where, when, how and in what manner, and touching other articles and circumstances in any wise concerning the premises, according to the tenour and effect of certain articles specified in a bill to these presents annexed. And therefore we command you that you attend diligently to the premises and do and execute the same with effect. And by the tenour of these presents we command our sheriffs of the counties aforesaid that at certain days and places, which you shall cause them to know, they cause to come before you or two of you as many and such good and lawful men of their bailiwick by whom the truth of the matter may the better be known and enquired of; and that you certify us in our Chancery of what you shall do in the premises in three weeks from the day of St. Michael next coming, together with this commission. In witness whereof, etc. Witness the King at Westminster, the 28th day of May.

(NOTE: similar letters are addressed to other Commissioners, directing them to make inquiries in other parts of the country.)

D. LORD DURHAM'S COMMISSION

[1838. From *Parliamentary Papers*, XVII, No. 3, 1839]

Victoria, by the grace of God, of the United Kingdom of Great Britain and Ireland Queen, Defender of the Faith. To Our right trusty and right well-beloved Cousin and Councillor, John George Earl of Durham, Knight Grand Cross of the Most Noble Order of the Bath, Greeting: Whereas, by five several Commissions under the Great Seal of Our United Kingdom of Great Britain and Ireland, We have constituted and appointed you, the said John George Earl of Durham, to be Our Captain General and Governor-in-Chief in and over each of Our Provinces of Lower Canada, Upper Canada, Nova Scotia and New Brunswick, and in and over Our Island of Prince Edward, in North America: And We have, by the said several Commissions, made provision for the administration of the government of Our said Provinces and of the said Island respectively, in the event of your absence, by authorizing the respective Lieutenant-Governors or Administrators of the Governments of the said Provinces and of the said Islands respectively, in that contingency, to exercise the powers by the said Commissions respectively granted to you: And whereas We have, by a Commission under the Great Seal of Our said United Kingdom of Great Britain and Ireland, constituted and appointed our trusty and well-beloved Henry Prescott, Esquire, Captain in Our Royal Navy, to be Our Governor and Commander-in-Chief in and over our Island of Newfoundland and its dependencies: And whereas there are at present certain weighty affairs to be adjusted in the said Provinces of Lower and Upper Canada: Now know you, That We, resposing especial trust and confidence in the prudence, courage and loyalty of you, the said John George Earl of Durham, have, of Our especial grace, certain knowledge, and mere motion, thought fit to constitute and appoint, and do hereby constitute and appoint you, the said John George Earl of Durham, to be Our High Commissioner for the adjustment of certain important questions depending in the said Provinces of Lower and Upper Canada respecting the form and future government of the said Provinces: And We do hereby give and grant unto you, the said John George Earl of Durham, as such High Commissioner as aforesaid, full power and authority in Our name and in Our behalf, by all lawful ways and means, to inquire into, and, as far as may be possible, to adjust all questions depending in the said Provinces of Lower and Upper Canada, or either of them, respecting the Form and Administration of the Civil Government thereof respectively: And whereas, with a view to the adjustment of such questions, We have deemed it expedient to invest you with the further powers hereinafter mentioned: Now know you, That We do in like manner constitute and appoint you, the said John George Earl of Durham, to be Our Governor-General of all the said Provinces on the Continent of North America, and of the said Islands of Prince Edward and Newfoundland: And We do hereby require and command all Our Officers, Civil and Military, and all other Inhabitants of Our said Provinces, and of Our said Islands respectively, to be obedient, aiding and assisting unto you, the said John George Earl of Durham, in the execution of this Our Commission, and of the several powers and authorities herein contained: Provided nevertheless, and We do hereby declare Our pleasure to be, that in the execution of the powers hereby vested in you, the said John George Earl of Durham, you do in all things conform to such instructions as may from time to time be addressed to you for your guidance by Us, under Our Sign Manual and Signet, or by Our Order in Our Privy Council, or through one of Our Principal Secretaries of State: Provided also, and We do hereby declare Our pleasure to be, that nothing herein contained shall extend, or be construed to extend, to revoke or abrogate the said Commission under the Great Seal of Our said United Kingdom of Great Britain and Ireland appointing the said Henry Prescott Governor and Commander-in-Chief of Our said Island of Newfoundland, and its dependencies, as aforesaid: And We do hereby declare, ordain and appoint that you, the said John George Earl of Durham, shall and may hold, execute and enjoy the said offices of High Commissioner and Governor-General of Our said Provinces on the Continent of North America, and of the said Islands of Prince Edward and Newfoundland, as aforesaid, together with all and singular the powers and authorities hereby granted unto you for and during Our will and pleasure. In witness whereof, We have caused these Our Letters to be made Patent. Witness Ourself at Westminster, the Thirty-first day of March, in the First year of Our Reign.

By Writ of Privy Seal.

EDWARDS.

E. INDIAN STATUTORY COMMISSION

[1927. From *Parliamentary Papers,* Vol. XI, Cmd. 3568, 1929–30, pp. xiii–xv]

GEORGE R.I.

George the Fifth, by the Grace of God, of Great Britain, Ireland and the British Dominions beyond the Seas King, Defender of the Faith, Emperor of India, to

Our Right Trusty and Well-Beloved Counsellor Sir John Allsebrook Simon, Knight Commander of the Royal Victorian Order, Officer of Our Most Excellent Order of the British Empire;

Our Right Trusty and Well-Beloved Cousin Harry Lawson Webster, Viscount Burnham, Knight Grand Cross of Our Most Distinguished Order of Saint Michael and Saint George, Member of the Order of the Companions of Honour, upon whom We have conferred the Territorial Decoration;

Our Right Trusty and Well-Beloved Donald Sterling Palmer, Baron Strathcona and Mount Royal;

Our Trusty and Well-Beloved Edward Cecil George Cadogan, Esquire (commonly called the Honourable Edward Cecil George Cadogan), Companion of Our Most Honourable Order of the Bath;

Our Right Trusty and Well-Beloved Counsellor Stephen Walsh;

Our Right Trusty and Well-Beloved Counsellor George Richard Lane Fox, Honorary Colonel, the Yorkshire Hussars Yeomanry, upon whom We have conferred the Territorial Decoration;

Our Trusty and Well-Beloved Clement Richard Attlee, Esquire, Major, late South Lancashire Regiment;

Greeting!

Whereas We have deemed it expedient that the Commission for which provision is made in Section 84 A of the Government of India Act should forthwith be appointed for the purpose of inquiring into the working of the system of government, the growth of education, and the development of representative institutions, in British India, and matters connected therewith, and should report as to whether and to what extent it is desirable to establish the principle of responsible government, or to extend, modify, or restrict the degree of responsible government then existing therein, including the question whether the establishment of second chambers of the local legislatures is or is not desirable:

Now know ye that We, reposing great trust and confidence in your knowledge and ability, have on the advice of Our Secretary of State for India acting with the concurrence of both Houses of Parliament authorised and appointed, and do by these Presents authorise and appoint you, the said Sir John Allsebrook Simon (Chairman); Harry Lawson Webster, Viscount Burnham; Donald Sterling Palmer, Baron Strathcona and Mount Royal; Edward Cecil George Cadogan; Stephen Walsh; George Richard Lane Fox and Clement Richard Attlee to be Our Commissioners for the purposes aforesaid:

And for the better effecting of the purposes of this Our Commission, We do by these Presents give and grant unto you, or any three or more of you, full power at any place in Our United Kingdom or in India or elsewhere in Our Dominions to call before you such persons as you shall judge likely to afford you any information upon the subject of this Our Commission: and also whether in Our said Kingdom, or in India, or elsewhere in Our Dominions to call for information in writing; to call for, have access to and examine all such books, documents, registers and records as may afford you the fullest information on the subject, and to inquire of and concerning the premises by all other lawful ways and means whatsoever, including the appointment by the Commission with the sanction of Our Secretary of State for India, of any person or persons to make subordinate enquiries and to report the result to the Commission:

And We do by these Presents authorise and empower you or any of you to visit and inspect personally such places as you may deem it expedient so to inspect for the more effectual carrying out of the purposes aforesaid:

And We do by these Presents will and ordain that this Our Commission shall continue in full force and virtue, and that you, Our said Commissioners, or any three or more of you, may from time to time proceed in the execution thereof, and of every matter and thing therein contained, although the same be not continued from time to time by adjournment:

And We do further ordain that you, or any three or more of you, have liberty to report your proceedings under this Our Commission from time to time if you shall judge it expedient to do so:

And Our further will and pleasure is that you do, with as little delay as possible, report to Us under your hands and seals, or under the hands and seals of any three or more of you, your opinion upon the matters herein submitted for your consideration:

Given at Our Court at Saint James's the Twenty-sixth day of November, One thousand nine hundred and twenty-seven; in the Eighteenth Year of Our Reign.

By His Majesty's Command.

W. JOYNSON-HICKS.

GEORGE, R.I.

George the Fifth, by the Grace of God, of Great Britain, Ireland and the British Dominions beyond the Seas King, Defender of the Faith, Emperor of India, to

Our Right Trusty and Well-Beloved Counsellor Vernon Hartshorn, Officer of Our Most Excellent Order of the British Empire,

Greeting!

Whereas We did by Warrant under Our Royal Sign Manual bearing date the Twenty-sixth day of November, One thousand nine hundred and twenty-seven, appoint Commissioners for the purpose of inquiring into the working of the system of government, the growth of education, and the development of representative institutions, in British India, and matters connected therewith, and of reporting as to whether and to what extent it is desirable to establish the principle of responsible government, or to extend, modify, or restrict the degree of responsible government then existing therein, including the question whether the establishment of second chambers of the local legislatures is or is not desirable;

And Whereas a vacancy has been caused in the body of Commissioners appointed as aforesaid, by the resignation of Our Right Trusty and Well-Beloved Counsellor Stephen Walsh;

Now Know Ye that We reposing great confidence in your knowledge and ability have on the advice of Our Secretary of State for India acting with the concurrence of both Houses of Parliament authorised and appointed and do by these Presents authorise and appoint you the said Vernon Hartshorn to be one of Our Commissioners for the purposes aforesaid, in the room of the said Stephen Walsh, who has resigned.

Given at Our Court at Sandringham; the Seventh day of December, One thousand nine hundred and twenty-seven; in the Eighteenth year of Our Reign.

By His Majesty's Command.

W. JOYNSON-HICKS.

F. ROYAL COMMISSION ON LICENSING (ENGLAND AND WALES)

[1929. From *Parliamentary Papers,* Vol. XI, Cmd. 3988, 1931–32, pp. iii–v]

GEORGE R.I.

George the Fifth, by the Grace of God, of Great Britain, Ireland and the British Dominions beyond the Seas King, Defender of the Faith, to

Our Right Trusty and Well Beloved William Warrender, Baron Amulree, Knight Grand Cross of Our Most Excellent Order of the British Empire;

Our Trusty and Well Beloved:

Sir John Pedder, Knight Commander of Our Most Excellent Order of the British Empire, Companion of Our Most Honourable Order of the Bath;
Sir Edwin Forsyth Stockton, Knight;
Thomas George Arnold, Esquire;
Eleanor, wife of Alfred Barton, Esquire;
Walter David Bentliff, Esquire;
George Alexander Bryson, Esquire;
The Reverend Henry Carter;
Allan Andrew Hart Findlay, Esquire;
James Fitton, Esquire;
Gerald Ashburner France, Esquire;
Benjamin Tom Hall, Esquire;
William Lionel Hichens, Esquire;
Arthur Jenkins, Esquire;
James Joseph Mallon, Esquire;
John Morgan, Esquire;
Edith Neville, Spinster;
Arthur Sherwell, Esquire;
Shena Dorothy, wife of Ernest Darwin Simon, Esquire;
Thomas Skurray, Esquire; and
Francis Pelham Whitbread, Esquire;

Greeting!

Whereas, We have deemed it expedient that a Commission should forthwith issue to inquire into the working of the laws relating to the sale and supply of intoxicating liquors, and into the social and economic aspects of the question, and to examine and report upon proposals that may be made for amending the law in England and Wales in the public interest:

Now know ye that We, reposing great trust and confidence in your knowledge and ability, have authorised and appointed, and do by these presents authorise and appoint you the said William Warrender, Baron Amulree (Chairman); Sir John Pedder; Sir Edwin Forsyth Stockton; Thomas George Arnold; Eleanor Barton; Walter David Bentliff; George Alexander Bryson; Henry Carter; Allan Andrew Hart Findlay; James Fitton; Gerald Ashburner France; Benjamin Tom Hall; William Lionel Hichens; Arthur Jenkins; James Joseph Mallon; John Morgan; Edith Neville; Arthur Sherwell; Shena Dorothy Simon; Thomas Skurray and Francis Pelham Whitbread to be Our Commissioners for the purposes of the said inquiry;

And for the better effecting the purposes of this Our Commission, We do by these Presents give and grant unto you, or any five or more of you, full power to call before you such persons as you shall judge likely to afford you any information upon the subject of this Our Commission; to call for information in writing; and also to call for, have access to and examine all such books, documents, registers and records as may afford you the fullest information on the subject, and to inquire of and concerning the premises by all other lawful ways and means whatsoever;

And We do by these Presents authorise and empower you, or any of you, to visit and inspect personally such places as you may deem it expedient so to inspect for the more effectual carrying out of the purposes aforesaid:

And We do by these Presents will and ordain that this Our Commission shall continue in full force and virtue, and that you, Our said Commissioners, or any five or more of you, may from time to time proceed in the execution thereof, and of every matter and thing therein contained, although the same be not continued from time to time by adjournment:

And We do further ordain that you, or any five or more of you, have liberty to report your proceedings under this Our Commission from time to time if you shall judge it expedient to do so:

And Our further will and pleasure is that you do, with as little delay as possible, report to Us under your hands and seals, or under the hands and seals of any five or more of you, your opinion upon the matters herein submitted for your consideration.

Given at our Court at Sandringham the thirtieth day of September, one thousand nine hundred and twenty-nine, in the Twentieth Year of Our Reign.

By His Majesty's Command,
J. R. CLYNES.

GEORGE R.I.

George the Fifth, by the Grace of God, of Great Britain, Ireland and the British Dominions beyond the Seas King, Defender of the Faith, to Our Trusty and Well-beloved Robert Thomas Jones, Esquire,

Greeting!

Whereas We did by Warrant under our Royal Sign Manual bearing date the Thirtieth day of September, One thousand nine hundred and twenty-nine, appoint Commissioners to inquire into the working of the laws relating to the sale and supply of intoxicating liquors, and into the social and economic aspects of the question, and to examine and report upon proposals that may be made for amending the law in England and Wales in the public interest:

And whereas a vacancy has been caused in the body of Commissioners appointed as aforesaid by the resignation of Our Trusty and Well-beloved Allan Andrew Hart Findlay, Esquire:

Now know ye that We reposing great confidence in your knowledge and ability have authorised and appointed and do by these Presents authorise and appoint you the said Robert Thomas Jones to be a Commissioner for the purposes aforesaid, in the room of the said Allan Andrew Hart Findlay.

Given at Our Court at Sandringham; the Third day of January, 1930; in the Twentieth Year of Our Reign.

By His Majesty's Command.
J. R. CLYNES.

G. NEWFOUNDLAND ROYAL COMMISSION

[1933. From *Parliamentary Papers,* Vol. XIV, Cmd. 4480, 1933–34, p. ii]

Dated 17th February, 1933. GEORGE R.I.

George the Fifth, by the Grace of God of Great Britain, Ireland, and the British Dominions beyond the Seas King, Defender of the Faith, Emperor of India: To Our Right Trusty and Well-beloved Counsellor William Warrender Mackenzie, Baron Amulree, Knight Grand Cross of Our Most Excellent Order of the British Empire, one of Our Counsel learned in the Law, Our Trusty and Well-beloved Charles Alexander Magrath, Esquire, Doctor of Laws, and Our Trusty and Well-beloved Sir William Ewen Stavert, Knight Commander of Our Most Excellent Order of the British Empire, Greeting.

Whereas on the advice of Our Ministers in Our United Kingdom of Great Britain and Northern Ireland, in Our Dominion of Canada and in Our Island of Newfoundland We have deemed it expedient that a Commission should issue forthwith to examine into the future of Newfoundland and in particular to report on the financial situation and prospects therein.

Now know ye that We, reposing great trust and confidence in your knowledge and ability, have authorised and appointed and do by these presents authorise and appoint you the said William Warrender Mackenzie, Baron Amulree, Charles Alexander Magrath, and Sir William Ewen Stavert, to be Our Commissioners for the purposes of, and to make, such enquiry.

And We do hereby authorise and require you with all convenient despatch and by all lawful means to enter upon, and to collect evidence respecting the subject matter of, such enquiry and to suggest such measures as may appear to you best calculated to meet the situation.

And We do further require you to conform in all things to such instructions as shall be addressed to you by Us.

And We do hereby charge and command all whom it may concern that according to their respective powers and opportunities they be aiding to you in the execution of this Our Commission.

And, for the purpose of aiding you in your enquiries, We hereby appoint Peter Alexander Clutterbuck, Esquire, on whom We have conferred the Decoration of the Military Cross, to be Secretary to this Our Commission.

Given at Our Court at Saint James's this Seventeenth day of February, One Thousand Nine Hundred and Thirty-three in the Twenty-third Year of Our Reign.

H. PAGEANT OF PARLIAMENT

(Suggestions for the Same)

[Printed by special arrangement with author and publisher from *Mild and Bitter*, Doubleday, Doran & Co., copyright 1936, 1937. First printed in *Punch*, Vol. 186, June 27, 1934, p. 708]

I saw an old man in the Park;
I asked the old man why
He watched the couples after dark;
He made this strange reply:—

"I am the Royal Commission on Kissing,
Appointed by Gladstone in '74;
The rest of my colleagues are buried or missing;
Our Minutes were lost in the last Great War.
But still I'm a Royal Commission
Which never has made a Report,
And acutely I feel my position,
For it must be a crime (or a tort)
To be such a Royal Commission.
My task I intend to see through,
Though I know, as an old politician,
Not a thing will be done if I do.

"I never can remember how exactly we began,
But I seem to recollect a case about a clergyman;
A mountain was delivered, rather strangely, by a mouse;
There were meetings, there were articles and questions in the House;
The necessity for action was clear to everyone,
But the view was very general that nothing could be done,
And the Government courageously decided that the Crown
Should appoint a score of gentlemen to track the trouble down—
Which always takes a long, long time.

"We first explored the history of human osculation,
The views of the Mohammedans, the morals of the nation,
And the significance (if any) of existing legislation—
And that took a long, long time.

"Next a little doubt arose about the limits of our reference,
We accordingly approached the Government with deference,
Having ascertained that kisses were of every kind and sort—
Some kisses, for example, being long and others short—
Did the Government expect us to investigate the latter?
The Government replied that it didn't really matter—
But that took a long, long time.

"Disraeli was a member, but he very soon resigned;
Lord Arrow died in '98, old Rattle lost his mind;
Still, once a month, in winter, we assembled to discuss;
And then the Boer War broke out, which interrupted us—
And that took a long, long time.

"We then collected evidence, but carefully dismissed
The opinion of anyone who actually kissed;
We summoned social workers from the cities of the North,
Good magistrates from Monmouth, Nonconformists from the Forth;
We summoned all the bishops who were over sixty-one
And asked if they were kissed and, if they were, how it was done.
They answered in the negative and said there was abundant
Support for the opinion that the practice was redundant—
And that took a long, long time.

"We next examined doctors with extremely high degrees,
Who thought that osculation was the cause of Bright's Disease,
And one or two Societies existing to suppress
All frivolous activity, including the caress;
Industrial employers said that kissing always tends
To economic conduct and is bad for dividends.
Just then the Great War happened; our proceedings were adjourned;
Two members joined the constables and seven were interned.
And I think that it was during that unfortunate campaign
Our Minutes must have vanished—they were never seen again—
For the War took a long, long time.

"There were ten of us surviving at the finish of the War,
And some of us were not so energetic as before;
But the sense of civic duty still invigorated all
And we gathered once a quarter in a cellar in Whitehall.
(These things take a long, long time.)

"One little question puzzled us for many a weary year:
'What is the right procedure when the Minutes disappear?'
The Secretary said he thought the precedents were small,
The Chairman said he didn't know a precedent at all.
The Secretary thought we should remember where we were
And continue our inquiry, without prejudice, from there.
But a lot of time had passed since the inquiry was begun,
And none of us remembered what exactly we had done.
And it has to be conceded that you can't go very far
Towards a definite objective if you don't know where you are.
The Chairman took the view that we should just begin again,
For the absence of the Minutes would be awkward to explain.
We resolved it was a question we could not at once decide,
And that was the position when the Secretary died—
But it all took a long, long time.

"That left the members seven. I should hate to call to mind
The melancholy steps by which our membership declined;
I know that on the suicide of Prebendary Gunn
I suddenly discovered that our membership was one.
And that's the reason why you may observe me in the spring
Investigating park-seats and places where they cling.
That kissing is proceeding there is very little doubt—
I can't imagine why it's done or what it's all about;
But whenever it's discovered that the plebs are having fun
It's generally granted that something should be done.
Civic duty's food and drink to me, and, though it may be
short,
I can promise you at least a unanimous Report—
But it does take a long, long time.

"I am the Royal Commission on Kissing,
Appointed by Gladstone in '74;
The rest of my colleagues are buried or missing;
Our Minutes were lost in the last Great War.
But still I'm a Royal Commission,
My task I intend to see through,
Though I know, as an old politician,
Not much will be done if I do."

INDEX